TEDDY
THE **JUMPS** IN MY LIFE

CONTENTS

El Quetzal
Guatemala's National Bird
(Photo courtesy of Carlos Iván Restrepo Jaramillo [IG: cirestrepo])

Perhaps my life story and my words will reach just the right individual, the right little boy or girl or adult, to inspire them to find their gifts, just as I did over so many years. My life has been rich with experiences, in terms of both extreme challenges and extreme rewards. Through these experiences, I have become conscious not only of the world and what it has to offer but also what must come from within. This awareness makes me both happy and sad. Happy to have lived, survived, and thrived. Happy to have influenced and taught so many. Sad because there are so many more to teach, to reach.

Compelled by the extreme difficulties of my own youth, it is my sincere, heartfelt desire to inspire, encourage, and lead others, *especially children*, to persevere and have hope through difficult times. Furthermore, I pray that my story will bring awareness about how empathy and random acts of kindness could make an absolute difference to a person when in the midst of one of life's agonizing or seemingly unbearable struggles.

If, by some chance, publishing my story helps even just a few people to overcome their struggles, either through having hope and persevering or by someone being more empathetic and helping them, then I will be happy.

So, it is to the children—of Guatemala and of the world—that I dedicate this book.

PUBLISHER'S NOTES

This book is based on Teddy's original autobiographical writings, along with extensive personal stories and accounts told by him.

Please note that the quality of some of the pictures may be poor. This is because for some of them, the original was not available.

CHAPTER ONE

How Could this be Happening to Me?

Watching super athletes Usain Bolt and Michael Phelps setting world records at the Beijing 2008 and London 2012 Summer Olympics on TV took me back in time. With a smile on my face, I began to reminisce about one of the most memorable times of my life.

In 1958, Mexico hosted the III Encuentro Internacional del Club Venado competition. Guatemala's Autonomous Sports Confederation (Spanish translation: Confederación Deportiva Autónoma de Guatemala [CDAG]) sent me to compete in the high jump event, which was the first time I ever formally represented Guatemala internationally. This marked the beginning of many competitions and many firsts in my life, including one other very important first. But more on that later!

Since this was my first time traveling outside Guatemala, my coach surprised me by taking me to the Sports Palace store (a sporting goods and retail clothing store), where he bought me a suit and tie, making sure I was presentable for the trip. When I saw myself in the mirror, I thought I was looking at someone else! I couldn't believe what I was seeing—me, a tall man in a suit, looking strong and sophisticated. Not only was it my first suit, it was also the first time I remember feeling like I was just a little bit good-looking; my confidence grew!

Although it was very intimidating, I went alone to Mexico, as the confederation did not authorize any expenses for my coach to travel with me. When I arrived in Mexico City, I checked into the hotel; it was the first time I had ever even stayed in a hotel room. Never in my life had I felt a bed so smooth, so perfect. I felt unworthy to sleep in it, thinking I should sleep on the floor instead. But curiosity prevailed, and I decided to sleep on the bed. Amazing! I had no idea a bed could feel so good. It was like nothing I had ever experienced—a far cry from sleeping on the ground in Guatemala or on an army bunk. I thought I was dreaming before I even fell asleep, and when I woke up the next morning, I felt incredibly energized.

On the day of the competition, the stadium was very crowded, yet I felt alone and isolated because, unlike my practice area back home in Guatemala, I did not know anyone there. When I saw athletes from Puerto Rico, the United States, Mexico, and many other countries, it added to my anxiety. I noticed the other athletes all jumped the Western roll style as they practiced, and they all had nice uniforms and shoes. I waited in the jumping area, wearing a generic shirt and a pair of shorts and, of course, *no shoes*. All these differences made me feel self-conscious, but I prayed and maintained my focus by concentrating on bringing home a win for Guatemala. While I was practicing, waiting for my turn to jump, a lady assisting the Mexican athletes approached me and told me that my shorts were too tight—that it would make it difficult for me to move my legs as much as I would need to. With my permission, she cut a slit up each side to loosen them. Although I was surprised by her gesture, I was grateful for her kindness.

The competition started, and after I made a few jumps, a Mexican athlete came up to me and asked, "Why don't you wear shoes to jump?" I simply told him I didn't have any shoes. An odd look came over his face; he was astonished I could jump barefoot. Then he did an amazing thing: he offered me his shoes, which appeared to have nails under them. When I put them on, I found it incredibly hard to walk normally; some people may have even thought I was drunk as I stumbled to get my balance. It was such a struggle that it made me laugh, thinking how silly I must look, and maybe because I was a little embarrassed. So I kept walking around until I got the hang of it, which didn't take very long. Once I got my balance, I felt stronger with each step.

Having the shoes gave me more confidence, but nothing made me forget my fears and feel more motivated, more invincible, and more alive than when I heard my name announced for the first time, with the name of my country: "Teodoro Palacios Flores, representing Guatemala." I wanted to make the Guatemalan people proud, so I did my very best to jump as high as possible. When it was my turn, I made the sign of the cross, as I always did, and started running toward the bar and as I jumped, it felt as though the shoes pushed me up. What happened next set the tone for the rest of my life and the rest of my challenges, which was to give my very best and always persevere despite adversities, inequalities, or lack of support.

With each go, I got more confident. By the time the rod was at 1.90 meters (6'2"), only a Puerto Rican and I remained in the competition, as all other jumpers had been eliminated. The bar was moved to 1.95 meters (6'4"). Despite the authorities saying no man could jump that high with that style, I easily jumped it, winning my first gold medal for Guatemala! My reporter friend, Fidel Echeverria, informed me that I had broken the world record of 1.93 meters (with the scissors style) established by William B. Page Jr. of the University of Pennsylvania of the United States in 1887.

None of the firsts I've mentioned so far compared to the first time I stood on a podium to receive a gold medal. In this surreal moment, I looked around at the anonymous spectators. The crowd was electrifying, clapping and cheering. I could not believe I was standing on top of the podium; it was a moment in time now burnt in my memory, and it was like nothing I had ever experienced, either physically or emotionally. My heart raced, sweat dripped down my face, and I was so excited yet so . . . Well, I do not know how to explain it. So proud yet so humble. I remember thinking, *How could this be happening . . . to me? Is this me, leaning forward as a gold medal is slipped over my head and now lies around my neck?* Glancing back, I saw the flag that symbolized more than just my home—it was where I belonged; it was a deep part of my identity. *All* my countrymen were my family. And in the middle of all that raw emotion, for just a few seconds, the little boy inside me wondered if my mom and my granny could see me from heaven. *Look, Mom. Look, Granny. Look what I have done. Look what I did for you and all of Guatemala. Are you proud?*

Taking all this in was almost too much. I was overwhelmed with these thoughts, all while listening to the beautiful sound of the Guatemalan national anthem. My emotions surged, and tears filled my eyes. For the first time, I felt that, through my jumping, I was bringing honor to all Guatemalans and, in particular, to all my family and the many people that helped me find my way during my difficult and lonely childhood. That's what fueled me and kept me jumping, event after event.

(Photo courtesy of Hector Xutuc Castillo)

This first event launched my jumping and athletic career, which lasted for the next thirteen years. After this first competition, I continued representing Guatemala in several national and international jumping events.

Mexico City, 1958
(Photo courtesy of CDAG)

CHAPTER TWO

The Foundational Years

Birth to Age Ten and a Half

I am proudly Afro-descendant Guatemalan Garifuna, born on January 7, 1939, in the town of Livingston, Izabal, Guatemala. My mother, Carlota Flores de Palacios, became ill and died when I was just two years old; I was her only child. I do not remember her, and in fact, I have never even seen a picture of her, although I have often wondered what she looked like. I imagine that I look like her and that the goodness that was in her is reflected in me. My father, Alejandro Palacios Nuñez, was unable to take care of me.

After my mother died, I went to live with my paternal grandmother, Catarina Nuñez de Palacios. She was so good to me, and I loved her very much. I called her Granny (*Abuelita* in Spanish), although as far as I was concerned, *she* was my mother. Granny took good care of me and always told me to be a good boy and to never disrespect people. She took the time to teach me basic good manners and morals. She also sent me to the local school, beginning in the first grade.

As far back as I can remember, the highlight of my week as a young boy was going to church with Granny. She was a very religious person; we never missed a Sunday. It was clear there was no compromising this activity, nor did I want to. Some of my early memories, around age five or six, are associated with going to church. It was then that I noticed how pretty Granny looked on Sundays. She definitely embodied the phrase "Sunday best" when it came to what to wear. The colors she wore were vibrant—reds, yellows, purples, teals—and they were all beautiful against her dark and weathered skin. If she had a coordinating hat, it was also part of the ensemble. Of course, she put me in *my* best clothes too, including a small black bow tie. I always felt special and proud when I wore my bow tie. Of course, it wasn't a perfect ensemble; I had no shoes, so I went barefoot!

When it came to Sunday church, Granny was serious, especially about being on time. As soon as we were dressed, we were out the door, walking briskly to church. Granny would frequently glance back at me to make sure I was keeping up. If I got too far behind, she would yell in a stern voice, "Teddy, hurry up now!" This was sometimes followed by her strong hand reaching back, taking a firm grip on mine to "help" me along. I never understood why we always had to walk so fast; we always seemed to be in a hurry. Were we perpetually late? Was I slow? I don't think so. Rather, I think it was her enthusiasm to get there—to be on time, to start socializing, and to be in a safe haven. Inevitably, we always made it with time to spare.

I was always happy to go to church. Although it was a simple church, it was a place of peace and beauty. I cannot remember much that the preacher said, but I remember loving the singing. After the service, we would stay so that Granny could mingle and talk to the other townsfolk, and I got to play with all the other children. Some of my fondest early childhood memories were when I was at church on Sundays.

One day after church, on our way back home, it started raining very hard, and it developed into a powerful thunderstorm. The wind blew forcefully, and we were pelted by the rain; it was so scary. But Granny pulled me close to her, and we took cover under a big tree, where we huddled together until the intense storm passed. When it was over, she looked down at me, wiped the water from my face, smiled lovingly, and calmly said we should be on our way again. Even at that young age, I remember feeling safe because Granny was protecting me.

The happy times with Granny ended far too soon. When I was eight years old, my sweet granny unexpectedly died. I didn't know how to cope with losing her or how to comprehend the impact. She was my protector, my rock, my world. My grief over losing her was tremendous, and it was a very hard blow for me because even though she was my grandmother, she was the only mother I knew, since I didn't remember my real mother. I am so thankful for my granny for taking care of me and for the early lessons I learned from her. I am especially grateful to her for taking me to church. I realize now that this was the beginning of my ethical and spiritual foundation, which paved the way for me to get through many difficult times. By attending church in those early years, I learned how to pray and to believe in God. After the church service, I learned to play with other children and was allowed to be a child. I learned to listen, to be on time, to respect people, and to strive to be good. And one more wonderful thing my granny did for me: she showed me what it felt like to be loved, and she told me how much my mother loved me too.

Nuestra Señora del Rosario (Catholic church
in Livingston, Izabal, Guatemala)
(Photo courtesy of Rodolfo Arana Flores)

I remember that suddenly there was a funeral at the house, common in small villages at the time, and there lay my beloved granny. Her passing happened so quickly, so unexpectedly, that I was seemingly in a state of shock. It was hard to comprehend, and I was so sad. In the midst of this sadness, I did not even think about who was going to take care of me or where I would live, but the next thing I knew, I was told I was going to be living with my aunt Felipa, my mother's sister.

Aunt Felipa Flores lived nearby and had her own children to raise by herself. The house was small; it had a kitchen area, and then there was one

7

big room where everything happened, from sleeping (all of us together in the same room) to eating and relaxing.

During the day, I continued going to school, where I completed the third or fourth grade, learning to read and write. It was a blessing that I learned those basics skills. Since I had to move a few times with Granny and Aunt Felipa, I did not get to finish a full school year. I attended the Escuela para Varones Justo Rufino Barrios in Livingston, where I was taught in Spanish. I also attended a rural school in Punta Gorda, Belize, where classes were given in English. Many people living in Livingston and Puerto Barrios would go to Belize so their children could learn English, because the United Fruit Company, a major employer with many jobs, required people to know English to get hired. This early foundation in the English language certainly served me well in my later life.

After school and chores, my cousins and I loved to play hide-and-seek, soccer, and other games outside until it was dark. Then Aunt Felipa would have us all sit on the porch across from the big room, where she demanded everyone's attention; she used this time to teach us about morality. At the time, I had no idea how important these lessons were. "You should *never* steal anything. Always listen and do *not* disrespect anyone. Gossip and lying are *not* allowed." She was extremely insistent about our actions around others. "If you are at another person's home, *do not* touch anything in their house, because you could break something. Always say thank you when you are given food or drink." One of the things she frequently insisted on was "You must always be obedient. If someone in authority tells you to do something, you should do it." Usually, toward the end of her talks came a warning: "You do not want me to *ever* catch you smoking or drinking." She said it with such conviction, with such a fierce tone, eyes slightly squinted and glaring, that I was truly afraid, but mostly afraid of how disappointed she would be with me. I was all ears, as I wanted to learn and show her respect. I took to heart the things she said, because only a few people ever took the time to teach me anything, so when she spoke, I listened. I was so fortunate to have been a part of her family.

Aunt Felipa would leave early every morning to wash, iron, and fold clothes to make a small living. She worked very hard to support us all, but it wasn't enough. There was very little to eat, and whatever food she managed to scrape together was always evenly divided among us all, even me. After dinner, I would sometimes see her secretly crying in the kitchen because she knew everyone was still hungry. She was kind to take me in, and I was so grateful for her; however, I could see her suffering, and I knew it was time for me to go. One morning, after breakfast, I packed a small bag with the few shirts and shorts I had and told her I was leaving. She said I didn't have to go, but I knew that I did. I told her I was sorry and that it was hard to leave. She hugged me tightly and sobbed quietly as she blessed me on my way out. Barefoot and lonely, I walked away.

I lived with Aunt Felipa for about two and a half years in total until I was about ten and a half. Even though I was still young when I left her house in Livingston, Izabal, my values were strong. Smoking, drinking, stealing, and bad behavior were out of the question; I never wanted to disappoint Aunt Felipa in any way, even if she never knew.

I was so lucky to have lived with Aunt Felipa, because living with her was like being in an ethics class. She shaped and molded my character by teaching me to be respectful, honorable, disciplined, obedient, humble, kind, and responsible; and both she and Granny taught me to always arrive on time. She also taught me that tobacco and alcohol were bad for my health, and the list goes on. I truly believe many successes in my life are thanks to my Aunt Felipa.

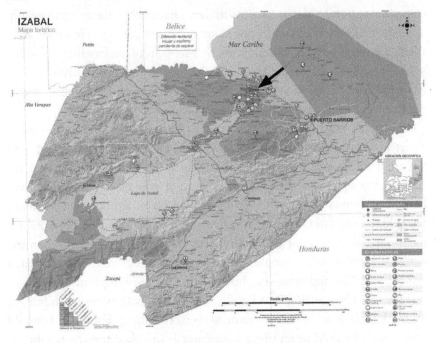

Map of Livingston County, Izabal, Guatemala
(Map courtesy of INGUAT) Instituto Guatemalteco de Turismo

CHAPTER THREE

Alone

Age Ten and a Half to Sixteen

Walking out of the door at Aunt Felipa's was hard, but it was nothing compared to how hard it became. With her, I had shelter, the companionship of a family, and some food to eat, albeit not quite enough. However, after I left, I learned what true hunger really was—and true loneliness. Oddly, what got me through these times was having already faced adversity and loss early in my life; losing both my mom and Granny unconsciously taught me to accept the unexpected and keep going.

So that's what I did—I kept going. I instinctively found my way to Puerto Barrios, one of the larger towns nearby, seeking work, food, and a place to call home. I do not recall exactly how I decided to go to Puerto Barrios, but somehow I was guided there. Not even eleven years old, I was living on my own in a town where I knew no one, although on occasion, I would see my father drinking in town. Although he never provided for me or looked after me, I still had pity for him. So when I saw him on the street, if I had a buck, I would sometimes give it to him so he could eat. I don't know if he appreciated it, but I knew I was helping him.

Shortly after getting into Puerto Barrios, my belly ached with hunger more than it ever had. The pain was excruciating. Even so, I would never steal; I would never disappoint Aunt Felipa, because she taught me better, and being without her made me appreciate her even more. I had no particular talents or skills, but I did have a strong mind, a strong body, and strong morals. That, along with the kindness and generosity of a few others, proved to be enough, to get by. Back then, being poor was more of a norm for many people in Guatemala. It wasn't unusual to see young children begging in the streets for money, food, or work. Unfortunately, the same is still true today.

Before long, my survival skills kicked in. I watched what other children did to earn a few coins, and I made friends with a few of the local boys. One of the first things I learned to do was polish shoes, a common job for the youth. This work was very inconsistent and barely provided enough money to cover a meal or two, but it was something to get me by here and there. Other times, I would go into a restaurant and ask to wash dishes in exchange for a plate of food. The owner of one of those restaurants, Mr. Brooks, would give me very large greasy stainless steel casserole pans to wash, which had the food baked or burnt on the sides. It seemed almost impossible to get them clean. Nonetheless, I scrubbed and scrubbed the pans with steel wool as hard as I could, sweating like I was in a sauna, until they were perfectly clean so that maybe he would let me come back again the next day. But I could not always find work, and there were many days I didn't have anything to eat. On those days, I scrounged in the trash for left over food, or depended on the generosity of my friends, who would offer to bring me a piece of bread with beans from their homes. I was always so thankful for the simple food; it was like a gourmet meal. The grinding in my stomach would stop, and I could relax for a few hours.

Since I didn't have a place to live, I eventually lost the few clothes I brought with me. I stayed in the same dirty clothes day and night. It didn't bother me so much because I was more concerned with eating every day and playing a little, but as one could imagine, it didn't take long in the hot Guatemalan sun to bake body odor into my shirt and shorts. That, combined with me sleeping on dusty or wet ground every night, made me look pretty grungy. There was an older lady named Mrs. Carlota who saw me on the street one day and asked me in a concerned way, "Boy, why are your clothes so dirty?" I explained that I was alone and homeless, and that they were my only clothes. Without hesitation, she reached out her hand and told me to come with her. For a moment, it made me think of my granny, when she would scoop me up by the hand to "help" me along on the way to church. Mrs. Carlota took me directly to her humble house, where she then gave me soap and a fresh towel, and told me to go take a shower while she washed my clothes—by hand, of course. When I was done, I kept covered with the towel, and she gave me some food. While I was eating, I watched her as she carefully pressed the clothes dry. As she ironed, she had a sweet yet serious look on her face. When she was done, she gave me the clothes to put on, and then she sent me on my way. This happened several more times when I would run into her in town, about every two or three months or so. In between my visits with Mrs. Carlota, I would bathe at the beach, just as many people of limited means did in those days. When my friends were there, I would sometimes take time to play and swim with them. In those moments, I was a very happy kid. What wonderful memories.

When I wasn't working in the day, I was able to make friends with a few of the local boys. One of them usually had a soccer ball, and we would find a place to play. I learned the game, and in no time at all, soccer became my favorite thing to do. I played as often as I could when I was not working. It was something that distracted me from the woes of my life; it was like the fulcrum that served to tip me back into balance when the seesaw of life had me down on the ground due to hunger or loneliness.

Night always came, and my friends went to their homes, where they were kissed good night and tucked into their beds. Not me, I would wander the streets late into the evening, kicking little rocks or a bottle around, wishing it was a soccer ball. Sometimes when people would see me in the streets long after dark, they would ask me what I was doing up so late. When I told them I was alone and homeless, occasionally I was offered to sleep on the ground in a corner of a person's house or inside their barn. I always accepted whatever was offered to me, never forgetting to say thank you. I knew Aunt Felipa would have been proud.

For the many nights when I wasn't so lucky, I found a place to go. I discovered two large woodsy trees where the Roy Fearon Stadium is now located. Every day, between five and six in the afternoon, I would go inspect the ground to see whether it was dry or wet under the trees. Depending on the situation, I would go back behind some of the buildings on the main street, where I usually found some cardboard box remnants. If the ground was wet from rain, I would bring as many as I could carry, using at least two or three to create a makeshift pallet to sleep on, saving one or two to provide a form of cover. I usually fell asleep easily, especially if I worked hard or played a lot of soccer that day.

Sometimes I would be in a deep sleep, only to be jarred awake by a loud clap of thunder or a startling rain. The only thing to do was to take shelter under the tree, crunch up into a ball, and hold any remaining cardboard over my head as a shield. I would remember when Granny held me tight during that frightening storm and how we just had to wait it out, but it was usually a long, uncomfortable night, as I would get soaking wet and quiver from the cold wind.

It was during these times that I believe my mind became conditioned to ignore physical discomfort and to push through a difficult, painful situation. I believe it also taught me patience, because in those situations, there wasn't much I could do except wait and hope that the sun would rise soon to dry my clothes and make me warm again.

I got lucky when it didn't rain at night. Lying on my pallet on the unclaimed plot of land I secretly called home, far from any lights of civilization, I would fold my hands behind my head for a pillow and stare at the brilliance above me. The stars were magnificent, and sometimes it seemed like they were so close I could reach out and grab one. My eyes would fixate on the thousands of flickering lights of various sizes and seemingly colorful flashes, with clusters of stars stretching across the entire sky—it was mesmerizing. It was common to catch a glimpse of a falling star, which was always exciting; it would then be a game to curiously wait to see another. I was emotionally moved by these scenes or when there was a beautiful full moon. It made me know that more was out there, and often it beckoned me to speak to God for answers.

"God, why did you take away my mother? Is she with you now? Can you tell her I need her?" I still longed to know her, to feel my mother's warm embrace and a loving kiss on the forehead, and to see her smile tenderly when she looked at me. "Is my granny with her? Do they miss me?" The night sky and solitude often gave rise to these kinds of thoughts and prayers. Sometimes I would cry because I missed them both so much, and the loneliness at times was almost unbearable, especially when I first left Aunt Felipa's. Without fail, I would find some comfort after praying, feeling as though my mother and Granny *were* looking at me from heaven, and I'm sure my granny was smiling for me. After all, she's the one who taught me to pray and helped build my spiritual foundation. I remember her telling me that God would answer my prayers, but I would have to be patient for an answer. At some point, I would drift off to sleep with a gentle wind blowing across my face, kissing me good night, relaxing me enough to get to sleep, knowing the sun would greet me in the morning—that constant of nature is what I could count on.

13

I rarely knew what, or if, I was going to eat that day, depending on whether or not I had a little money left over from the previous day. It was so much easier to forget about being hungry or alone when I could find a group of boys playing soccer at the park. I got lost in the game; all my senses and energy became focused on following the ball and making the plays. Of course, I was lean, so I was fast. The challenge, the interaction, the thrill of stopping the ball and of being good at something took my mind off my worries and made me feel happy. I subconsciously realized that if I played well, people wanted to have me on their team. A good player makes a game more fun, and of course, everyone likes to win. The more I played, the better I got. So I played whenever I could find a group, or even when I was alone if I could find or borrow a ball. I would play with the ball for hours, just kicking it against a wall so I could try to catch it just as goalkeepers do. Today they would call this practice in organized sports. For me, it was called the best part of my day!

As time passed, I found refuge in the Catholic church. There was one priest in particular, Father Santiago, who became a great influence in my life. In those days, there were many poor children; however, Father Santiago saw the depth of my poverty and needs, and he would give me something to eat from time to time. On one occasion, he saw me in very dirty and threadbare clothes, so he gave me an old white altar boy soutane, which I wore for the following few weeks. It was simple offerings like that that made a difference to someone like me, who had nothing. It was as if he knew what things to give me that would mean the most: food, cover, and perhaps most importantly, the dream to play soccer. You see, many boys went to church because Father Santiago would loan them a soccer ball. In fact, so many boys would come to play soccer that Father Santiago organized a soccer team called Juca. It was a great team, but I couldn't be part of it because I was too young. When they weren't practicing as a team, I played soccer with them when they would let me which helped me become agile and physically stronger, and helped me develop my soccer skills. These were some of the happiest moments of my early life because it was the first time I actually played soccer. It took my mind away from my troubles, my hunger, and my loneliness. I was instead filled with excitement, competitiveness, and comradery; I felt like a regular boy, like I fit in somewhere. It seemed so natural to play this sport. The more I played, the better I got; the better I got, the more I wanted to play. And the cycle continued until it was almost consuming. It was as if this was

14

the gift God gave me. As a young man, I would ask God to guide me to be the best goalkeeper Guatemala ever had. Looking back, perhaps that was not the right kind of *spiritual* prayer I should have been praying, but I believe soccer led me on a path to other successes in my life, knowing that one day my story would be told and that I would inspire and teach others.

Teddy the Fisherman

Despite my love and passion for playing soccer, which I would have loved to have done every minute of the day, many of the events in my youth were centered on finding something to eat. Oftentimes in the evenings, when the weather was right, some fishermen would gather at the pier at the El Rastro area around six o'clock. Piling into a small fishing boat, they would fish all night, with plans to return by six or seven o'clock the following morning. People in the local area would anxiously await their return to purchase the fresh fish they brought back. I wanted to fish with them because they always carried food, and I knew I would have something to eat. I would show up early, hoping to go, although at first they said I was too young. Even so, they let me go a time or two, and when they did, I worked hard to show them what I could do. Word got around about my high energy, obedience, and willingness to do whatever they asked of me, and soon I was welcome on several trips. Oftentimes the fishermen would pay me two or three bucks for helping to bait the hooks, clean the fish, and then unload and clean the boat when we got back. After some of the men understood my circumstances, they would give me a break and let me sleep on the boat for a few hours during the night. It was easy to fall asleep after working hard for several hours on a beautiful night, with the boat rocking me back and forth, putting me to sleep like a baby.

An enthusiasm for work naturally and quickly evolved in me, perhaps because my very survival depended on it. Of course, at the time, it wasn't work to me. I just did what had to be done. However, in very subtle ways, I recognized that when I worked hard, I got more opportunities, which meant more food, and generally, life was better.

Teddy the Baker

There was a man named Mr. Rafael Palencia who was the owner of a very good bakery in town. Mr. Palencia was a large man (a little rotund, you might say) with a delicate smile that would put to rest any fears about his character. If I was in the vicinity of the bakery, I would smell the delicious aroma of freshly baked bread and pastries, and inevitably, my mouth would water. Each time I passed in front of his store, I would salute him. I'm not sure why I did this; he just seemed to command my respect, and it brought a gentle smile to his face, breaking the monotony of working constantly. One day, I felt confident enough to go inside and ask him to teach me something so I could earn some money, promising to do the best job I could. When he saw I was being serious, he gave me a job. I was shocked. He was the first person to have helped me by teaching me a skill instead of just pitching me a piece of bread to eat—he taught me how to make the bread. It was also a lesson that you have to ask for what you want. Sometimes you get what you ask for, and sometimes you get even more!

Very soon, I learned to make many different kinds of bread. We would start baking early, around 4:00 a.m., and I was always on time, as I didn't want to let Mr. Palencia down. After baking for several hours in the early morning, I carried dozens of loaves of bread in a basket on my head, delivering them all around town. Doing this work made me feel proud, as I helped bake and then deliver bread to others to start their day. Mr. Palencia and his wife were happy with me too, as I was a very fast and courteous delivery boy. I became their favorite and was earning fifty cents a week, plus bread. Soon they raised my salary to one dollar a week and still allowed me to have bread and some pastries to eat. I worked diligently for them for many months. Then a friend told me of another bakery in town that offered much more pay. While I didn't want to leave my job with Mr. Palencia and his wife, the other job paid substantially more money—eight bucks per month, plus bread and other baked items, double what I made with Mr. Palencia. I spoke with Mr. Palencia about the other job and pay, but he could not afford to pay me that much. I took the other job, even though it was hard to leave. We all respected one another, as I left on good terms.

I enjoyed making and delivering bread. The new bakery hours were much longer than I was accustomed to, so I worked very hard to keep up and still do a good job; however, working constantly wore me down. I felt a calling to do something different, something very different. I wanted to play soccer—the desire just would not leave my mind. Was it a boyish, shortsighted desire? Was I being irresponsible or even lazy because I *knew* I had to have money to eat? I had so many questions, but I was no longer motivated by the bakery job; I think it was due to exhaustion. After contemplating for several days, I left my job at the bakery, wondering if I was making the right decision, worrying that I was walking away from the certainty that I would eat every week, all for the sake of playing soccer. It was not an easy decision, but I made it. In retrospect, I know it was not only the right decision, it was my destiny.

Soccer Was My Passion

When I heard the sound of a game in play or when I saw or heard a soccer ball bounce, I had to go play. From the early days of playing soccer with the boys at church, I was obsessed with the game. Initially, it took my mind off my worries and hunger pangs, and it was the only thing that reminded me I was a child. What's more, I seemed to be a natural and played well, probably because my body was lean and athletic from walking and working so much, which continuously fueled my motivation to practice and play.

My favorite position to play was the goalie, which I was very good at playing because I had great reach. Plus, it is a very important position because no matter what else happens on the field, the only way for a team to win is to score a goal. So I worked hard to keep the other team from scoring. Blocking most of the shots to the goalie and preventing a score always led to cheers by the coach, the players, and fans, or whoever was watching. I liked the praise and recognition, something that rarely came from any other source, and I found it to be very motivating.

When I was barely fourteen years old, I became the goalie of an adult team, the Esfuerzo. I'm pretty sure they did not know I was just fourteen, or I wouldn't have been allowed to play. Between being fairly tall at the time and having advanced soccer skills, they must have assumed I was an adult. The team was owned by a local Guatemalan man named Mr. Moncho. When he realized how poor I was and that I had no shoes to play in, he took pity on me. I will never forget it—he bought me my first pair of soccer shoes and a sweater. When I got them, I cried on the inside and smiled on the outside. OK, I cried on the outside a little too, but I was so happy to have something so nice. I loved my shoes and my sweater so much that I didn't want to take them off and would just go out and walk around with them on. I was very proud to be on his team. I worked very hard to show my appreciation.

Sunday never came fast enough, because that was the day we played soccer. I loved it when the other team shot toward the corners, because I had to leap on the ground, stretching to defend the goal and block the ball. It felt great when the attacking players passed the defensive players so I could jump on their feet and get the ball. It was my dream to become the best goalie ever in Guatemala. Anytime I was on the soccer field, I felt liberated, important, and in control for the first time in my life, and I left my worries behind. You could say it was not only my passion but also my escape.

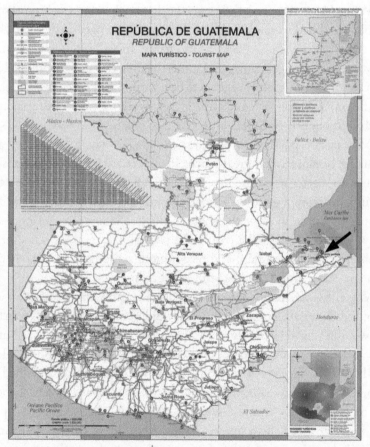

Map of Guatemala showing the eastern city of Puerto Barrios, Izabal
(Map courtesy of INGUAT)

CHAPTER FOUR

Teddy the Soldier

Age Sixteen to Eighteen

Time passed. My daily struggle to find food and shelter continued, managing one day at a time. I was still very passionate about soccer, especially the goalie position. One day while I was sitting on a bench in town by the El Rastro area, a friend stopped by to tell me that there was a soccer team at the military base and that they needed a goalie. He encouraged me to find out if I could become a soldier, because if I was accepted, I could live, eat, and play there. Wow, what a dream! Were my prayers being answered?

Without hesitation, the next day I went to the Puerto Barrios military base in El Rastro. After explaining that I was available and would make a commitment to serve the mandatory time, they immediately accepted me even though I was only sixteen years old. I started right away. It is difficult to explain how I felt being inside the base. I felt peace, security, and stability, like you do when you are at home, something I had longed to have ever since leaving Aunt Felipa's. Now I was in the military. For the first time since Granny was alive, I had my own bed and a place to be, and while there wasn't a family member there or the smell of warm pie cooling in the window, it was home. Finally, I didn't have to worry about food, clothes, or a place to sleep every single night. I was given two pairs of new boots and three uniforms to wear and keep clean. I was also given a rifle, a helmet that was quite heavy, a water jug, and a metal plate and mug that

I used when I ate. At last, I had clothes and things that belonged to me, and I remember feeling that all these things were such a luxury.

The first night, I slept peacefully. Military life started bright and early the next morning at five o'clock. Everyone jumped up, grabbed their soap and towel, and headed to the showers. Even getting a military shower was a blessing. After that was breakfast, then a host of marching exercises, and then instructions about how to be a good soldier. I loved the military, especially the instructions like "Present arms! Shoulder arms! Right flank! Left flank! At ease!" I loved the precision of the movements and the feeling that we were working together as a team. Of course, when we had free time, I played soccer. The captain of the team saw me playing and liked how I played so much that he made me the goalie of one of the teams at the base. It felt great!

Life was beginning to take shape for me in the military. I had a sense of belonging and contentment that had been absent from my life since leaving Aunt Felipa's, something I had missed for a long time. On top of that, I got to play soccer! I wanted to show my appreciation for my new life by doing well. So with great determination, I dedicated myself to learning the Soldier's Manual. Thank God I had learned how to read and write! Even though many nights I was tired from marching and physical exercises, after the lights were off and the other soldiers would fall asleep, I would lie on my stomach on the bed, clutching a flashlight with one hand and the corporal's instruction manual with the other, reading and studying until late in the night. Some nights the moon would shine so brightly in the window by my cot that I wouldn't even need the flashlight. I loved taking a break to stare at the moon; it always brought back memories of sleeping outside under the trees. It also reminded me to pray and talk to God.

All the soldiers were astonished when, after just a month and a half, I took and passed the corporal's test! This usually took a soldier about three months to accomplish. I continued to work hard, and after only five months in the army, I was a second sergeant, which usually took a soldier six months on average to achieve, although many of them had no self-motivation and never even tried. Being on my own for so long taught me that I had to push myself to overcome any obstacle in order to get what I wanted. Before the military, my life was mostly about striving for food and shelter. Now it was about doing well and earning respect.

Although I loved the success I was having as a soldier, I was still obsessed with soccer. I was very disappointed the day I was told that the captain in charge of the soccer team had been transferred to the military base of Zacapa. He had believed in me, and we had great rapport. I was sad to see my friend go, and I wondered what impact his leaving would have on my playing soccer.

One day while I was on guard duty, the new commanding officer, Colonel Luis Alfredo Ruano, arrived at the base. I saw him getting out of a car, and although he was about 5'6", his presence gave the impression of him being a tall, revered man. He was very serious-looking, projecting himself with all the confidence one could have. His movements were precise and exact, and he was meticulously clothed. Every single button on his uniform glistened like a star because they were all so shiny. His uniform was pressed to perfection, and his shoes were immaculately polished. Rumor had it that a prophet had arrived!

Several days later, I went to the soccer field at the base. There was the colonel, looking very different. He was still very professional and stoic, but he had transformed from his crisp military uniform to a striking soccer uniform—the kind I had only seen in newspapers and magazines. He was donned in a shirt with black-and-yellow vertical stripes and black shorts and socks. He was there playing soccer by himself, playing the ball with ease. I wanted to see how he played, so without interrupting him, I scooted behind the closest tree to carefully watch him.

Although I wanted to play too, I was scared I would be rejected, not because I wasn't a good enough player but because *I* wasn't good enough. Why? Because he outranked me, and I dared to be on the large field at the same time as him? No, in my mind, it was because I was a black man and he was Ladino. Maybe for the first time, I realized the color of my skin could dictate events in my life. I'm not sure why it hit me so strongly at that moment, but I feared the colonel would reject me. Of course, this was happening during a period where my self-esteem was very low; oftentimes, the other soldiers would have visitors or letters from home, and me, nothing.

Amid my self-doubt, suddenly the ball escaped the colonel, landing about twenty meters from me. Instinctively, I ran like lightning to catch it; all the while, my eyes were fixated on the ground, afraid to look up in fear of being told to get out. I picked up the ball and ran to the center of the goal and stopped. Little by little, I lifted my head while slowly opening my eyes to see his reaction. To my great relief, there was a smirky smile on his face, the kind where one side of the mouth is slightly higher than the other, as if he was pleasantly surprised, and there was a simultaneous slight up-and-down movement of his head. In a flash, his reaction transformed my fears and erased all my negative thoughts. I threw the ball back to the colonel, and he started smoothly shooting the ball at me, perhaps taking pity on me because I was still a very thin and undernourished young man. He noticed how I caught his shots easily, so he started shooting stronger. I told him to get closer and shoot the ball harder, shocking him. He moved in, sending it to the corners, challenging me more, which I loved. I blocked all the shots—he couldn't believe his eyes! Instantly, I gained his respect. From that day forward, the colonel and I had many more exchanges on the field, where we developed a mutual respect for each other. I would also see him in the mess hall, where he would say hello and give me a thumbs-up, and I would return his hello with a soldier's salute. Having this connection with the colonel made me more confident, so I kept playing on the military team; the colonel always enjoyed watching me play.

Months passed, and to my dismay, the colonel was transferred to the army base in Guatemala City. I'm sure this was a good move for him, but losing my friend at the base made me very sad. The colonel told me that I shouldn't worry, that he would send for me. However, before I heard from him, my tenure in the army ended, and I left without knowing anything about the colonel or his whereabouts.

Five months later, a friend from the army tracked me down with a message: the colonel was waiting for me in Guatemala City.

CHAPTER FIVE

The Glory Years

Age Eighteen to Thirty-One

I arrived in Guatemala City the following Monday, and Colonel Ruano was very happy to see me, welcoming me with open arms. Singing my praises, the colonel introduced me to Mr. Rubén Amorin, trainer of the military soccer club, officially the Aurora Futbol Club, where he reigned as coach from 1958 to 1971 and again later in 1984. The Aurora was a professional team owned by the Guatemalan army, and they were excellent, playing at a superior level.

To test my skills, I played in two unofficial Aurora matches in Guatemala, and then they offered to let me live in the Army Stadium at Campo Marte Park, in a very small room, which I did. Eventually, they added me to the Aurora team. It was tough, but I pushed myself to the limit, and the effort paid off, as I was warmly accepted by the other players. It was thrilling to play with such skilled players.

Soldiers from various military corps came to the stadium to train for different sports. I had gotten to know the army's athletic trainer, Mr. Cyril Victor Thomas, quite well. He knew of my hardships but liked and respected me. One day, he came to visit me, and he told me I was the prototype of an American athlete—tall, thin, and quick—saying I even reminded him of Jesse Owens when I walked. He suggested I practice other sports, but I told him soccer was my passion and was the only sport I was interested in playing. I couldn't imagine doing anything else. Not only was I very, very good at soccer, but it was the only sport I had ever played or even knew how to play. To think about trying other sports was daunting and made me feel insecure. I was content and confident in my ability to play soccer, and that was all.

Mr. Thomas did not give up so easily. He took great interest in me and showed that he cared. He frequently brought me things I could not afford, like fruit juice and milk and also food and cakes. He even altered some of his clothes so that they would fit me, and he sometimes invited me to his home for dinner or visits. All this helped me get stronger, both physically and mentally. I began to trust this man's advice because I felt he was sincere and would not lead me in the wrong direction. He became my mentor, teaching me to depend on others for advice.

Finally, I did as he suggested and started learning and practicing various other sports. One day while training for the high jump, I jumped 1.8 meters (5'9"). I knew the jump was good. Even I surprised myself, but not as much as I surprised the people around me; they couldn't believe it. Everybody was amazed! They measured the distance several times, thinking it was a mistake, but it was not. Then they called Colonel Ruano to show him how high I jumped. He, too, was shocked. That familiar sideways smile came over his face again as he said, "Teodoro, everybody here can kick the ball, but *none* of us has *ever* seen a man jump 1.8 meters. No more soccer for you!" Instantaneously, my destiny changed. It was bittersweet. The thought of doing something unique and being the best at it was electrifying, but the thought of leaving soccer behind was terrifying. My jumping made everyone happy except me. Inside, I was devastated to think of not playing soccer, but those early lessons my aunt Felipa taught me about being obedient and respectful had served me well and kept me alive so far. I knew what I had to do. I had to follow the instructions of my great mentor, Colonel Ruano. I stopped playing soccer with an ache in my heart.

Like most things I've done in my life, I *jumped* right into training in other sports, like the high jump, the long jump, and the 200-, 400-, 800-, and 1,500-meter track events. I also practiced the discus and the javelin throw. I competed in many events, and after winning various competitions, they eventually decided I should just concentrate on three of them. I immediately excelled in the high jump. I jumped barefoot because, well, I had no money for jumping shoes! I tried various jumping methods, but instinctively, I jumped with a scissor style, which was the most difficult method since you jump over the rod in a sitting form, meaning my body launched even higher in the air to clear the rod. It was just the most natural method for me, and it worked!

Guatemala City circa 1958
(Photo courtesy of CDAG)

Guatemala City circa 1959
(Photo courtesy of CDAG)

Guatemala City
(Photo courtesy of *Prensa Libre*)

Guatemala City
(Photo courtesy of *Prensa Libre*)

Guatemala City
(Photo courtesy of *Prensa Libre*)

High Jump Career

1958

(See chapter one for full details of 1958.)

When I returned to Guatemala from Mexico, I was awarded with the military's first-class sports medal. I thought it would be the first of many awards from the military; however, it was the first and only award, as well as the first and only time my friends and the press ever saw me wearing the army uniform.

The military's first-class sports medal
Guatemala City, 1958
(Photo courtesy of *Prensa Libre*)

1959

I was very busy and had a great year in 1959, with many competitions, medals, trophies, and studies.

At the Central American and Caribbean Games in Caracas, Venezuela, I won the gold medal, which was the only medal won by the Guatemalan delegation. This was very special because not only did I win the gold medal, but I also won it on my birthday, January 7! What a great present, considering that for most of my life until that point, I had never received a gift or recognition of any kind on my birthday!

In Guatemala's national competition, I won three gold medals and one silver:

- Gold for the high jump at 2.06 meters
- Gold for the long jump for 6.57 meters
- Gold for the pole vault at 3.19 meters
- Silver for the 4×400 relief with a time of 3:48:04

At the III Pan American Games, held in Chicago, I narrowly missed the podium, placing fourth. Even though I didn't get a medal, this event was incredible because not only was I competing among and learning from the best jumpers in the world, but I also had the honor of meeting the great American Olympic athlete Charles Dumas, who was the first athlete in history to jump seven feet. After he won first place in the high jump event, we spent some time talking, and he gave me some jumping tips. I also had the great opportunity to meet Billy Mills (William Mervin Mills), the only American who later won the 10,000-meter run at the 1964 Tokyo Olympics. He is a member of the Oglala Sioux Tribe. We had a great conversation about our cultures' challenges; he is such a great, humble man.

I had the privilege of meeting the incredible Jesse Owens; I was in awe of this great athlete. I said to him, "You know, over the years, I have been told a few times that I walk like you." With a grin, he quickly replied, "Oh, I'm sorry to hear that!" We continued to joke and talk sports. After a short visit, we said our goodbyes, going our separate ways. But then he turned around and yelled back to me, "Keep up that great walk and the high jumps!" It was a surreal encounter, especially when I think about how it was only a few years ago that I was a boy living homeless in the streets of Puerto Barrios, Guatemala. Now here I was, shaking hands and talking to one of the greatest athletes of all time.

Teddy (*left*), Jesse Owens (*center*)
Chicago, 1959
(Photo courtesy of Teodoro Palacios Flores)

Teddy at the top of the podium
Guatemala City
(Photo courtesy of *Prensa Libre*)

In addition to my sports training and competitions, I attended English classes at IGA (Instituto Guatemalteco Americano), where I obtained my certificate to teach English as a second language (ESL). Learning English was not difficult for me since I spoke a bit of it when I attended elementary school in Belize. I also learned Garifuna from Granny; it is the language most folks speak at home in Livingston. With Spanish, the primary language in Guatemala, I'm lucky to speak three languages!

After my graduation, I was offered a job there to teach English, which I happily accepted. It was an ideal situation because it gave me time to keep training in the day while earning a salary at night. It was a small salary, but it was enough for my food and shelter; anything I had to spare was sent to my aunt Felipa, for whom I am forever grateful for all her love, care, and advice.

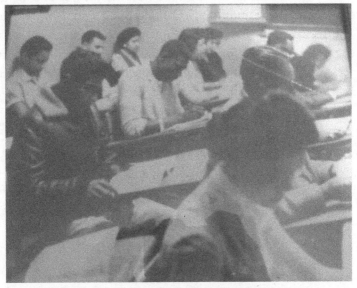

Teddy taking classes at the English institute IGA
Guatemala City
(Photo courtesy of Teodoro Palacios Flores)

I moved from the Army Stadium to a nearby room, also in Campo Marte, where the army had many small hotel-like rooms for soldiers who came for training or other activities. The rooms were in the shape of an L, and the walls were made of wood planks, many with gaps between the planks. Now this didn't bother me except when it rained, because my bed and other things would get wet, like the small AM radio I kept next to my bed. The radio kept me company and gave me something to do at night. I loved listening to sports or news broadcasts into the night, oftentimes until I fell asleep.

One evening while I was lying in bed and listening to the radio, it began to rain. Looking around my room, searching for a solution, I noticed the stack of my medals, trophies, and plaques piled up in a corner, which triggered a thought: *Why not use these?* Since I had no other materials, I hung the plaques and some of the medals over the gaps in many areas. It worked! The rain barely came in, and I could at least get to sleep without getting wet.

When my friends from Puerto Barrios would come to the city, they would ask me if they could sleepover at my small humble room, and of course, I would let them; I knew all too well what it was like *not* to have a place to sleep. Over time though, I noticed the rain coming in a little more, and I soon realized some of my medals and plaques were missing! I suppose they became someone's souvenirs. I never questioned my friends about it; I was just happy to provide them with a place to stay. Besides, I knew how many events I won, and so did Guatemala!

Guatemala, 1959
(Photo courtesy of *Prensa Libre*)

1960

A lot happened in 1960. I was invited to participate in the first Ibero-American Games in Chile. The Autonomous Sports Confederation of Guatemala refused to provide me with any expense funds other than a hotel and an airplane ticket to go to Chile to represent Guatemala. Therefore, I sold my suit for a few bucks even though it cost a lot more originally, and I went to Chile, where I won the gold medal. Then I was invited to compete in two other events and won two more gold medals, all without a coach. I was the first man to jump more than two meters in South America, which electrified the audience. They were cheering and applauding, and I was so connected to the crowd, lifting both my arms to wave back at them. By the time I won my second medal, I felt so much love and respect from the people of Chile as they kept cheering for me. It was truly an honor to be appreciated. I always acknowledged and thanked the crowd, finding it easy and enjoyable to engage with them. Still, each time I accepted a medal and the Guatemalan anthem would play, I longed to have my countrymen there with me to share the victory.

Because of these winnings, I was then invited to compete in Brazil, but I had no more money. I asked one of the delegates from the Autonomous Sports Confederation who was also there in Chile if I could borrow a few bucks, but he refused. I missed the opportunity to compete in Brazil. Disappointed but with my head held high, I boarded the plane to go home from Chile, proud to have honored my country with three gold medals. I fell asleep and dreamt of a great homecoming; maybe a band would be playing, with lots of people eagerly waiting, and maybe even a government official would be there to congratulate me. I woke up as we touched down at the Guatemalan airport and quickly situated myself to be alert and ready, but I was not ready for what happened next. Nothing. To my dismay, when I deplaned, there was no band and nobody waiting to greet me or congratulate me. In fact, there was no one there to give me a ride from the airport.

Certainly they were just late, and someone would soon be coming to pick me up. I waited and waited and waited, hoping to see a friendly face pull up and wave me to their car. Day turned to night, and it was closing time at the airport; I was told I couldn't stay inside anymore. This was one of those times that hit me hard emotionally, because I had nobody, no money, no food, and no way to get home. I remember thinking how ironic it was that just a few hours earlier, I was being cheered and applauded and was excited to get home and share the good news. Instead, with a heavy heart and an ache in my belly, I resorted to asking a baggage handler at the airport if he could spare ten cents just so I could catch a bus to my room at Campo Marte. He graciously gave me the money, and I headed back home, carrying my old traveling bag full of shiny medals and trophies for no one to see.

The lack of acknowledgment and appreciation was hard to accept because I had witnessed the enthusiasm and support other athletes received from their countries for the same, or even less, accomplishments. Even with the sting of no support, I had many beautiful and unforgettable happy memories. There is nothing like competing and winning, which I experienced many times. No matter how much I made Guatemala shine while I was in another country, at home in Guatemala it didn't seem to matter to the government officials. This was baffling to me, and I know it registered somewhere deep in my psyche. Years later, some reporters asked me, "How come when you practice here in Guatemala, you struggle to jump over two meters, but when you compete abroad, you do it with ease?" All I could say was that I was energized by the crowd and competition, and I wanted so badly to make Guatemala proud. Every trip was a chance to bring home a win for my country, and one more chance they might appreciate what I accomplished.

I became frustrated with the lack of support and acknowledgment, and basically with being ignored and discriminated against, which led to me getting into an argument with a military official. I was arrested by an army officer and sentenced to a few months in jail, even though everything I said about not being supported was true. My question was, Why? Was it because I was a very poor man or because I was black? No other athlete from Guatemala had nearly as many achievements, yet mine were never acknowledged. The only support I received was emotional support from Colonel Luis Alfredo Ruano, friends, reporters, and my trainer, who was unable to travel with me because the Autonomous Sports Confederation of Guatemala wouldn't pay for his expenses.

After I was released from jail, I went to Xela in Quetzaltenango, the second largest city in Guatemala, where many people gathered to see me perform the high jump at the Mario Camposeco Soccer Stadium. I jumped 2.10.05 meters, setting a Guatemalan national record that stood for the next fifty-seven years. I believe part of the reason I did so well there was that when I got arrested, I kept myself busy exercising in my cell, so when I left I was in great shape. Setting a national record was such an emotional moment that made me cry of happiness and accomplishment. They measured the bar to confirm it, but still, some folks disputed the record and wanted it removed.

Also in 1960, I was sent to represent the Guatemalan army in the department of Alta Verapaz, Cobán, Guatemala, to compete there at the Monja Blanca Stadium. As I was getting off the plane, a Catholic high school musical band started playing. *Finally, a hero's welcome*, I thought, feeling honored and happy, smiling back at the kids. The teachers of the school that knew me came over to greet me, and after the band stopped playing, all the kids ran to me to say hello and shake my hand. The huge smile on my face dimmed a bit once I learned they were instead expecting a bishop on that flight, which was why they were there. Even so, because I was already a celebrity in the newspapers and TV, they were still happy to see me and started playing the band and took pictures with me. The bishop had missed the flight, or maybe I was just lucky!

1961

I was invited to represent Guatemala at the World Indoor Championship at Madison Square Garden in New York City. Once again, I went there alone, without a coach and without anyone to advise me about the particulars of travel or competition, all of which was very intimidating. It was incomprehensible to me that the Autonomous Sports Confederation of Guatemala would send me to New York City, the capital of the world, to represent my country with no support from them. I recall sitting by myself in a corner, waiting for my turn to jump, looking all around at over 16,000 spectators, thinking how everything seemed so big yet I felt so small. It was a struggle to be there by myself, but at the same time, I was used to struggling in life, as I had been by myself since I was a kid. With the fierce competition of the reigning world champion, Valeriy Brumel from Russia, and John Thomas, the American favorite, I never thought I would get a medal. I noticed how they both had a constant flow of handlers taking care of their needs before, during, and after a competition. They brought them food, took them sightseeing, and organized their events, like banquets and practices. They even had interpreters, not to mention official uniforms and official practice wear. But as usual, when I heard my name and that I was representing Guatemala, I became instantly motivated and focused. Brumel and Thomas placed first and second respectively. I proudly achieved third place, receiving a bronze medal. I often wondered, if I had had the type of support other athletes got from their governments, what might have been possible for me? For Guatemala?

Valeriy and I became good friends. He invited me to go to Russia to train with him to learn techniques to improve my jump and to compete there. I couldn't believe that this white man, a world champion with so many world records, including a silver medal in high jump in Rome at the 1960 Summer Olympics (and later in 1964, a gold medal at the Tokyo Summer Olympics), would shake my hand, have a conversation with me, and respect me enough to invite me to train with him in his home country. Valeriy once said that "in sport, there is no Kremlin and no Wall Street. There are only athletes."

Teddy shaking hands with world champion high
jumper Valeriy Brumel from the Soviet Union
Madison Square Garden, New York City
(Photo courtesy of *Prensa Libre*)

Excited by the opportunity to work with the world champion of high jump, I asked the Guatemalan government to please allow me to go to Russia to train with Valeriy, because without their financial support, I could not go. I was given no response to my request.

Afterward, I competed in many cities in the United States and Canada, including Boston, Philadelphia, Peoria, Baltimore, Buffalo, Chicago, Toronto, and Winnipeg. In all competitions, I won a medal alone, without help or support, either from a coach or from someone to guide me during my travels.

During the 1960s, the United States was in the midst of a civil rights movement involving a lot of controversial, sometimes violent, race and desegregation issues; so it was not easy or sometimes even safe for a black man to travel alone in the United States. After a competition one evening in Baltimore where I had won a medal, several athletes decided to go into town and find a place to have some food and a drink. We found a bar that also served food, and we went in. However, the owner stopped us as soon as we were in the door and told us his bar was not integrated and he would not serve me. Being the only black athlete in the group, I felt awful and embarrassed. In my mind, there was nothing for me to do but go back to the hotel. I turned to leave, and as I did, to my surprise, the other athletes supported me. Without a scene, everyone left, and we went back to the hotel together. Their actions meant the world to me.

1962

I had a great year in 1962. It was a very successful and special year for me; I participated in and won many competitions both nationally and internationally.

I planned to go to the United States to train to improve my high jumping skills so that I would be prepared to compete at the Olympics in Tokyo, Japan, in 1964. My Guatemalan sports trainer, Mr. Cyril Victor Thomas, helped me get established with Coach Ellwood Johnson, a trainer at a university in Pennsylvania whom I had originally met in Chicago in 1959 at the III Pan American Games. In order to be allowed to train with him in Philadelphia, I needed my discharge paperwork from the Guatemalan army, which I requested. Although they complied, I was only given a license for one year, to stay until the end of 1962, with an option to extend the license for another year *if* I improved. I had neither money nor financial support from the Autonomous Sports Confederation of Guatemala, the Guatemalan government, or a private sponsor; but Mr. Johnson had seen me perform in competitions and recognized my potential. He not only arranged a scholarship for my training in Philadelphia, but he also helped me get a job at the Juvenile Center for Crime Prevention. What's more, Mr. Johnson also provided me a room in his own house to live in during my scholarship. I was so amazed by his sincerity and generosity. I treasured the opportunity to be trained by him, and I will always remember his kindness and support.

In August, the Central American and Caribbean Games were held in Kingston, Jamaica, where athletes came to compete from all Central American countries, including Mexico, Venezuela, Panama, Colombia, Cuba, Jamaica, and the Antilles—fifteen nations in all. Although I was clearly the best candidate to represent Guatemala due to my training, travel experience, and record of wins, the Autonomous Sports Confederation of Guatemala required me to compete with my countrymen in order to qualify to go to Jamaica. By this time, many Guatemalans were aware of my successes, so literally thousands of people gathered to watch me compete at the stadium in Guatemala City.

I did not disappoint them. I jumped 2.02 meters even though I had difficulties passing the bar with my left leg, something my trainer worked on with me to improve. The people loved me and were amazed to see me jump. I felt very happy to see so many Guatemalans cheering for me; it made me proud to be supported by them and only served to reinforce my drive to win. Needless to say, I was selected to participate, but again, very little aid was provided by the Autonomous Sports Confederation of Guatemala.

Lack of support showed even in the smallest of ways. With no allowances for equipment, improvising was necessary, but living on the streets as a youth had taught me to be resourceful. When I was practicing, I used a pickax to loosen the dirt where I landed, since I had no actual equipment to cushion the landings to prevent injury (as depicted in the following photo).

Teddy
Guatemala City
(Photo courtesy of Teodoro Palacios Flores)

At the Central American and Caribbean Games held in Jamaica, I got the gold medal and broke my high jump record at 2.0 meters and established a new record since 1926 in Jamaica. This was no easy feat! I trained very seriously for these games because the Jamaican competitor, Ernle Haisley (Ernest Leighton Haisley), was a fierce competitor and had beaten me in 1959 in Chicago at the III Pan American Games, winning the bronze medal and leaving me in fourth place. The thought of that experience fueled me to push myself harder during training because I knew I was capable of beating him. Having been together at many competitions, Ernle and I had become great friends. Oftentimes, we used to joke and laugh before games, but once the games started, we were respectful competitors. Right after the award ceremony, he said to me, "I should have let you beat me in Chicago so you could have let me win here with my people." To which I replied, "Don't forget, they are my people too!" I was so thankful for those happy times; we had great laughs and mutual respect.

While in Jamaica for the competition, several of us went to a party one evening. I used to love to dance and go out with the other athletes. The next morning, I was sanctioned by the Autonomous Sports Confederation of Guatemala; they suspended me from competing for a few months. I acknowledged that I deserved the sanction, but what bothers me is that the Autonomous Sports Confederation of Guatemala was all too happy to sanction me without hesitation, though they rarely did anything to support me, either with money, a uniform, shoes, or coaches, when I did compete. I desperately wanted to look like the other athletes who wore their country's uniform, especially the official team jacket, usually with the flag of their country and sometimes their name on the front and back. I used to dream that one day the Autonomous Sports Confederation of Guatemala would give me one of those jackets, but year after year, the dream never came true.

We were about thirty-one athletes returning from competing in Jamaica, where we had won seven medals: two silver, four bronze, and my gold medal. When we got off the plane, we were delighted to be greeted by a colonel representing the president and a band playing, including the marimba, in our honor. That was awesome, but the most wonderful moment was seeing my great friend Mateo Flores waiting by the plane door to welcome us home and congratulate us on our victories.

The second Ibero-American Games were held in Spain in October 1962, an event where athletes from all Spanish language countries, plus Brazil and Portugal, competed, around seventeen nations in total. I won another gold medal. Because of this, I was then invited to compete in Germany, where athletes from Argentina, Brazil, Colombia, Chile, Peru, and Venezuela were competing. I rode with some athletes who were also going to the competition in Germany. Unlike athletes from other countries, I had neither a proper uniform nor proper shoes with which to compete. My shoes were the ones I used both in practice and in competition, and they were worn out. Despite these disadvantages, I remained focused on winning for Guatemala and conquered another gold medal in the high jump at 2.01 meters.

After winning the competition, the German athlete Wolfgang Schillkowski, who won second place at 1.98 meters, came up to me, and using a translator, he said, "I never thought you were going to beat me wearing those old worn-out shoes. You have my respect and admiration, and please accept this as a gift." With that, the German gave me two pairs of his shoes, which appeared to be practically new. The words and the gesture made me so emotional and thankful for this fellow athlete. It was interesting to me that I always received so much respect and support from athletes and people from other countries, but not so much from my government.

Receiving awards was always a thrill for me. I always felt a moment of glory, freedom, respect, and love when I was standing at the top of the podium, hearing the Guatemalan national anthem play, with the flag displayed because of me. In front of over 26,000 spectators in Ludwigspark, Germany, I received a standing ovation; I felt like a superhero and couldn't believe their response.

I carpooled back to Madrid with the same athletes, only to be faced with the fact that I had not been given a return ticket to go back home to Philadelphia, where I was staying for training purposes. The president of Guatemala at the time had promised to wire the money for my return, but it never arrived. With only about two dollars in my pocket, I went to the Spanish Olympic Committee to ask for a ticket to Philadelphia. They were kind and provided me with a plane ticket to New York City instead, though I would have to find a way back to Philadelphia. By the time I got to the New York International Airport / Idlewild Airport (later renamed John F. Kennedy International Airport following John F. Kennedy's assassination in 1963), I remember I was so hungry despite being given a little food on the plane. It immediately brought back the memories from my youth. After arrival at the airport, I had to unexpectedly pay over a dollar for taxes and fees, leaving me only twenty-five cents, more or less, for train fare to get home to Philadelphia, which was only enough to get to the train station at the border of Pennsylvania. With no choice, I bought the ticket, got off at the border of Pennsylvania, and started walking. I wasn't afraid, because I had the advantage of an athlete's strength and stature. Even with a few lifts along the way, I walked for over three hours in the cold to finally make it home.

It made me sad to have been in such a wonderful big city, having won gold medals from Europe but having no money with which to eat or travel. I used to wonder if the Autonomous Sports Confederation of Guatemala or the government did not want me to represent Guatemala anymore. After all, it wasn't the first time they had left me on my own.

In Guatemala, an athlete of the year is selected by the government. It is one of the most distinguished honors in the nation, typically given to the athlete with the most merits nationally and internationally. There were several years when I knew I had been the best athlete to compete both nationally and internationally, yet the title was given to others who accomplished far less. This was never more obvious than in 1962, when I was absolutely certain the Athlete of the Year award would be mine. Instead, they chose an athlete who hadn't even competed internationally. *Unbelievable!* They said I was "undisciplined," never explaining their accusation. It was *very* hard to accept this blame since I had so many victories while receiving so little support. How is it that I was considered undisciplined when I was sent to Europe without a coach, a guide, practice clothes or a uniform, proper shoes, money, or a return ticket to the United States or Guatemala, yet I brought back two gold medals. Incredible!

The disappointment was both real and confusing. It would seem to me that of all the great men that voted for the Athlete of the Year award in 1962, someone, if not several people, would have stood up to dispute the vote or would have argued the facts of the medals and accomplishments. I had served my country in the military and was now serving my country by pushing my body and performing athletically at a superior level. Yet no one—not a single person—fought for me, for my merits, or for the medals I brought home. Nothing, absolutely nothing was offered or contemplated. In my opinion, both then and now, it was a theft of the greatest magnitude. And they got away with it because I did not have the leverage of any politician or even a family member—no mother, no father, no one to fight on my behalf—allowing them to look the other way without reprisal.

1963

I won four medals in 1963 in the US and Canada: one gold, one silver, and two bronze.

Fidel Chavarria, a reporter who was a good friend of mine, recalled the following: "I remember the day we came back from competing in the Pan American Games in Sao Paulo, Brazil. Teddy brought home a silver medal, and other Guatemalans—José Azzari, Cesar de la Vega, and Francisco Sandoval—also had great performances. Only our good friend, Ms. Sandra Samayoa Serovic, was waiting for us at the airport in Guatemala with a bucket of flowers. While we were happy to see at least one person that cared, it was so disappointing that the athletes were neither supported nor welcomed by our government."

1964

After intense training for the past two years and many international competitions, I was in my prime, and I knew I was ready, both physically and emotionally, to compete at the 1964 Olympics in Tokyo. The Autonomous Sports Confederation of Guatemala claimed there was no budget to send anyone. I begged them to send me, promising to work harder than ever, but they refused. I do not know why I was so surprised; they also did not send me to the 1960 Olympics in Rome, where the gold medallist won the high jump at 2.16 meters. Interestingly, in my jumping career, I achieved 2.14 meters, 2.16 meters, and 2.18 meters. If they had accepted my talent and given me just a little support, maybe Guatemala would have had its first Olympic gold medal in 1960 or even in 1964. How motivating it would have been to the people of Guatemala; I can only imagine that it would have ignited interest and enthusiasm in sports, resulting in more athletes competing and potentially more Olympic medals. Over fifty years later, the Guatemalan government still spends millions to get an Olympic gold medal.

But I soon learned the heartbreaking truth. I overheard a few of the officials from the Autonomous Sports Confederation of Guatemala say, "What a pity he is black. Otherwise, we could have done something to send him to the Olympics." Not being allowed to go to the Olympics was one thing, but hearing this was devastating; it came close to crushing my spirit. I considered giving up the sport, never jumping again, because I realized it didn't matter how hard I trained or that I was the best athlete in Guatemala. Hurt and frustrated, I lashed out, telling some people how I felt. Word got around, and I soon learned that some of the authorities at the Autonomous Sports Confederation in Guatemala wanted to kick me out of the delegation so that I would never again compete in an international competition. They didn't like hearing me grumble, even though I only spoke the truth.

After I got over the shock of that experience and accepted that all I could do was my best, I continued on my journey quietly, knowing the truth would eventually come out. The rumors settled down, and they did not prevent me from competing in future events.

During that year, I was able to take the English proficiency exam so I could continue to teach English at night.

Teddy's English certificate
1964
(Photo courtesy of Teodoro Palacios Flores)

1966

During the Central American and Caribbean Games in Puerto Rico, I won the gold medal. After I returned home, Gaspar Pumarejo, a TV host from Puerto Rico who also hosted a show in Guatemala from 1964 to 1966, asked me if I liked Puerto Rico, and I said, "Of course, I love your beautiful island." In appreciation for representing Guatemala, he offered me a free trip to visit the island and to be a guest on his TV show while I was there. I gratefully accepted, as this was one of the few times I had ever received any recognition. During the interview, I did not hesitate to openly and publicly express my heartache over never having been supported or recognized for my achievements by the Guatemalan government. I would never lie; I only spoke the truth. However, after being on the show, the sports delegation authorities in Guatemala were outraged and once again threatened to kick me out so that I would never again compete in an international competition. And once again, they did not follow through.

1968

By the time the 1968 Olympic Games of Mexico came around, I was not in peak physical condition to compete in the Olympics, because the focus of my sporting career had shifted to basketball. Even so, they invited me to compete and gave me the honor of carrying the Guatemalan flag in the opening ceremony, as my merits were well-known by then and beyond those of any other Guatemalan athlete. Plus, perhaps, the government may have done it in response to my claims that they had never supported or recognized me.

The '68 Olympics happened during a time where racial tensions were ignited not only in the United States but also globally and leaked into world competition events like the Olympics. It happened that two black US athletes, whom I did not know personally, put on a black glove each during their award ceremony and raised their hands, displaying a peaceful protest against racial discrimination. Their actions became world news, and a journalist asked me what I thought about their protest. I answered that if they were protesting against all the injustices suffered by black people due to the color of their skin or heritage, then I didn't see anything wrong with wearing a black glove; in fact, I understood them very well because I had personally been a victim of discrimination for being black as well. I had read about slavery and was aware of other racially discriminating acts in other parts of the world, where black children were not allowed to go to white children's schools, where black people had to sit in the back of buses even if the front seats were unoccupied, and where in 1963, John F. Kennedy had to send the Alabama National Guard to the University of Alabama so that black students could register for school, among many other injustices. After that interview and without asking me any questions, the representatives from Guatemala's Autonomous Sports Confederation came and took the flag away from me.

This action affected my mindset for the upcoming high jump trials. Besides not being at the top of my game physically, this caused me to be mentally distracted as well. As a result, I did not advance past the trials. However, at this Olympics, I had the privilege of meeting Dick Fosbury (Richard Douglas Fosbury), an American high jumper who made history in those games and who is considered one of the most influential athletes in the history of track and field. Besides winning the gold medal at the 1968 Olympics, he revolutionized the high jump event with a back-first technique, now known as the Fosbury Flop, which has been adopted by almost all high jumpers today. His method was to sprint diagonally toward the bar, then curve and leap backward over the bar, which gave him a much lower center of mass in flight than traditional techniques. I had competed in many high jump events using various styles, including the Western roll, the straddle technique, and the scissors jump, so it was exciting to witness a great new technique.

Where Was the Recognition?

I could keep writing about my odyssey, as there are so many little stories similar in nature, but I believe the message has been documented. I conclude this part of my story by saying that I represented my country in many competitions around the globe with heart and obedience for Guatemala. I recall winning the following gold medals:

- Five gold medals in Mexico
- Five gold medals in the USA
- Four gold medals in Panama
- Four gold medals in Honduras
- Four gold medals in Costa Rica
- Three gold medals in Chile
- Two gold medals in Puerto Rico
- One gold medal in Venezuela
- One gold medal in Jamaica
- One gold medal in Spain
- One gold medal in Germany
- Forty gold medals in Guatemala

And I held the Guatemalan national record for the high jump—2.10.05—for fifty-seven years, until 2017.

No matter what country I competed in, for me, there was nothing more beautiful and special than seeing our flag at the top. Regardless of where I was, I was always deeply moved when accepting a medal on behalf of my beloved Guatemala. Tears always rolled down my face every time I stood on the podium and heard the Guatemalan national anthem. In those moments, it was truly less about me and more about bringing honor to Guatemala.

I spent roughly thirteen years competing for Guatemala, and not even a radio worth five bucks was given to me as a prize by the Guatemalan government. The one and only award I received in Guatemala was the first-class military sports medal given to me by a military general at the army base in recognition of my many athletic talents, ranging from high jump to soccer.

Basketball Career

I found that the kid in me loved all sports, especially the ones with a ball. I first became interested in basketball when some friends took me to watch a professional game after jumping training one day. One of the professional basketball coaches at the national gymnasium in Guatemala, Noél Illescas Palacios, offered to teach me the rules and strategy of how to play the game; he subsequently became my mentor and coach. I had played basketball as a kid living in Puerto Barrios, but not very serious, just to be able to hang out with the boys. With practice and determination, in no time at all, I owned the court and could dunk the ball. Of course, being 6'3" made it easy for me to play, although I couldn't have advanced my game without Noél Illescas Palacios. Thanks to him, I was soon playing in the first division of basketball in Guatemala City. When playing with the first division team, I was lucky to have a uniform, something I never had when I was competing in the high jump.

I played basketball for over eight years with the military team in the major league in Guatemala City, Leones de Marte. The games were attended by many people and were oftentimes broadcasted on the radio.

When I first started playing basketball, I still competed in various high jumping events. Jumping gave me great satisfaction because I knew I was good at it. I won medal after medal, putting Guatemala in the spotlight, but was oftentimes still alone at the competitions. Basketball was different; I loved being part of a team. My teammates knew of my other accomplishments and had great respect and admiration for me. Their acceptance and comradery gave me something I hadn't had in a very long time—the sense of family and belonging I had always sought. I did not feel so alone anymore. Oftentimes after a game, we would all go get something to eat and rehash the game, especially when we won. Those were great times, and they meant so much to me.

Another reason I liked basketball was the fans! They followed the game so closely as we moved up and down the court. As soon as I scored, which I often did, I would lift my hands and wave them back and forth to motivate the crowd. In seconds, the fans would be on their feet, cheering and celebrating; their energy gave me a huge rush. They made me come alive—the more they cheered, the more I connected with them, the more I wanted to hear it again. Getting that appreciation felt good, so I worked hard to improve my plays. Whenever I got the chance, I would watch American basketball games on TV to learn new techniques and then practice them. It was easy to see that dunking the ball got a lot of attention, so I did that as often as I could!

We won many championships, some year after year. I was a natural at the game, and of course, I always played each game wholeheartedly. However, as the years passed, the coaches started keeping me on the bench more than on the court. For a time, it was confusing to me because my basketball skills had only improved with time. Oftentimes I got a lot of attention from people who knew me because of my international high jump accomplishments. It wasn't long before I saw the connection: the more people fussed about me, the more I warmed the bench!

One day, the Flores brothers asked me to join the team Hercules, assuring me I would actively play and not sit on the bench. That commitment sealed the deal, and soon after, I was on the court doing what I knew how to do: play with my heart and soul. We did great in the year 1969, more or less, and the last game of the season was for the championship. Incredibly, the opponent was none other than my former team, Leones de Marte!

Now this game in particular was the most memorable basketball game I ever played. The score was tight throughout the game, and then at the end, it was tied until the last few seconds. Then *wham*! I scored the last two points, and we won the championship against the guys who had kept me on the bench. My teammates whisked me onto their shoulders, parading me around the basketball court while the fans were cheering and screaming "Ted-dy! Ted-dy! Ted-dy!" This was an unforgettable moment for me. I felt so alive, so appreciated.

I also had the privilege of playing with the Guatemalan national basketball team. I had many great moments as a player of this team, and I was always proud to once again represent my country. I truly have had some thrilling basketball moments in my life.

Years later, in 1993, I happily served as a volunteer staff member of the second World Maxibasketball Championship, held in Las Vegas, Nevada, where I assisted with the logistics of the tournament. Watching some of the games took me back in time to the thrill of the last championship game.

Este es el campeonísimo quinteto masculino "Leones de Marte" en 1964. En el orden usual y atrás: Norman "Buco" Ramírez, Jorge Mario "Conejo" Dighero, Gonzalo "Pajitas" Villavicencio, Jorge Letona y Ruben "Rata" Ocaña. Adelante mismo orden: Teodoro Palacios Flores, René "Palo" Rivera, Ernesto "Sen-Sen" Miliàn, Juan José "Conejo" Argueta y Jeremías Stokes (q.e.p.d.)

Teddy and basketball team Leones de Marte
(Photo courtesy of CDAG)

Teddy and the Guatemala national basketball team
(Photo courtesy of CDAG)

Teddy and the Guatemala national basketball team, third place
Panama, 1962
(Photo courtesy of CDAG)

CHAPTER SIX

A New Start in the United States

Age Thirty-One to Sixty-One

My strength has carried me though my life. Let me explain.

I had relied on my *physical* strength to provide for my needs for most of my life since age ten, first to work long hours to have enough to eat and then later to strive to be the best athlete for Guatemala. At thirty-one, my physicality peaked, and I could no longer compete at the top level. With deep sadness, my sports career came to an end in 1970. When I announced I was retiring to my friends, teammates, reporters, and others, they were shocked and encouraged me to continue playing. However, with an ache in my heart, I explained to them that I had to find a full-time job to make a living and move on, fighting back the tears and sadness.

Then I was jobless and needed to find work, but it was difficult because there was little opportunity in Guatemala, especially for someone with little schooling or real work experience. Despite having achieved so much, it seemed my life was going in a circle, landing me right back where I was before my athletic career began. Familiar childhood feelings of being lost and alone crept in, taking me back in time. A feeling of depression lurked over me, and frankly, I just did not know what to do next. I began going out to meet some friends at a local bar, and before I knew it, I started drinking. I just wanted to forget that I had no job and no other opportunities. This lasted for about two months, until one night, in desperation, I cried out to God for help. Old lessons from attending church during my youth rushed to my mind. I prayed for answers and for God to help me understand my path. It was now time for me to rely on my *spiritual* strength. Before long, amazing things began to happen.

Back in 1963, when I was in Brazil, I had met a man named Edward M. "Ted" Haydon (1912–1985), who was a coach at the University of Chicago and the founder of the university's track club. He was inducted into the USA Track & Field Hall of Fame and the US Track & Field and Cross Country Coaches Association Hall of Fame. He participated as an assistant coach at the 1968 and 1972 Summer Olympic teams and the 1963 and 1979 Pan American Games (source: Wikipedia). He was a man of intelligence and heart, not to mention someone who had connections and knew how to get things accomplished. We had subsequently met in New York during other competitions, and in 1965, I had the privilege of being trained by him for a few months in Chicago, where we worked mostly on improving my jumps. Mr. Haydon provided me with so much support at that time, emotionally and technically. Moreover, he never showed me any kind of discrimination. I was blessed to have had the opportunity to be taught by such a great man, and I am forever grateful for Mr. Haydon.

During my travels to the United States, I saw that in spite of the racial tensions during that time, there were many opportunities for people to become educated and work. Remembering this, I wrote Ted a letter asking for help to get to the United States. I was amazed by how quickly he replied, sending me an airplane ticket and a letter to give to the United States Ambassador in Guatemala. Thanks to Mr. Ted Haydon and his response, I stopped drinking and started concentrating on what I had to do to follow his instructions to travel to Chicago. *Wow!* Before I knew it, I was in the United States. Another prayer answered! Mr. Haydon offered a lot of support and advice about how to make a living and get established as a resident. However, one thing he forgot to tell me was which Chicago neighborhoods to avoid!

My first job was to go door-to-door to sell products from a catalog. I was so excited to start work. I packed a satchel with catalogs and some samples to show and demonstrate. I guess the man who hired me really wanted to test me, because he sent me to sell in the projects, where there was a lot of drugs, prostitution, and gun violence. Less than a day on the job, a couple of drug dealers approached me, calling me names and insulting me. I thought it best not to fight them alone, so I looked down and said I was only trying to make a living and that I would only continue if they gave me permission. My submissiveness seemed to appease them, but they still searched my body, satchel, and clothes, emptying my pockets and taking the few dollars I had. Then they told me I was "cool" and I could go into the project buildings. After that day, I saw them a time or two as I continued to work the area, but no one bothered me. It was as if we had a mutual respect for the territory. To the surprise of many, including both my boss and myself, I was the top seller my first month and received a good commission. I asked two other salesmen, "Why has no one been to those buildings to sell our products?" Responding with shock, they said, "Are you crazy? No one wants to go there—it is far too dangerous. We don't know how you did it!" It didn't take me long to realize that working that territory was a huge risk to my well-being. When other grown men who knew the area were afraid of it, it made me afraid as well. After that, there was no way I could keep working in that area, so I left that job.

I had another job working at a grocery store where customers placed their order at the front counter, then waited while their order was filled. My job was to take the order, fill it, bring it to the front, and then ring up the order so the customer could pay for it. This was a commission-based job, so I worked very fast.

One of my co-workers was a blond lady named Marilyn, who was a single mother and always in need of money. Her mom took care of her children so she could work, and oftentimes her mom would call to speak with Marilyn about something that was going on with the kids. When the store phone rang, anyone nearby would answer it. Many times, I picked up the phone and instantly knew when it was Marilyn's mom, as it wasn't unusual to hear a kid crying or fussing in the background or just the distress in her mom's voice. I would call Marilyn to the phone. Without fail, as she took the phone from me, I could see her in my peripheral vision wiping the phone clean before using it.

I could see her struggle and her difficulty in trying to work and still deal with issues at home. Even though she felt the need to clean the phone after I used it, I had compassion for her situation because I could see she was honest and a hard worker. Because of the frequent distractions, both in terms of time and focus, her sales suffered. Sometimes when I had a big order for a customer, instead of me ringing it, I gave it to Marilyn to ring so she could take the commission. I know that the first time I did it, Marilyn was in disbelief of what was happening. She knew instinctively what I was doing though, because the sweet look on her face and gentle smile said thank you. I remembered how I had received unexpected kindness so many times, and this was my way to be supportive of her in her time of need.

It had been about three months of me giving Marilyn an order or two a day, when one day the phone rang. I answered it, and it was Marilyn's mom. As Marilyn took the phone from me, I saw that this time she did not clean it. I did a headshake in surprise. After the call, I asked, "Today you did not clean the phone?" She immediately broke into tears, hugged me, and said she was sorry. It was a special moment for me, not only because I was seen as her equal but moreover so because I saw her grow in her humanity that day by overcoming some of her racial biases. Of course, I instantly forgave her. From that day forward, she greeted me with a hug every morning, and she never again wiped the phone when I gave it to her.

I worked a short stint at a Laundromat, where my job was to fold and count bedsheets. It was tedious work, and an eight-hour shift felt like sixteen hours most days. One day I was busy folding, and I guess my mind drifted to memories of soccer or jumping, because I fell asleep for a few minutes and forgot to count the sheets. The next thing I knew, the supervisor fired me. Whew, what a relief! I normally would have been sad to be fired because that would have felt like rejection, but not this time. A folding and counting job was not for me.

After that, I took a job working with mentally challenged children. On a beautiful day in Chicago, we took the children for a walk to play at a large nearby park. Everything was going well until we had to move to another side of the park. It was then that we noticed one of the children was missing. We quickly scanned the park, but the child was nowhere in sight. It was terrifying. I mean it's one thing when you are scared about something having to do with yourself, but when it is another person, especially a child with special needs, it's a whole new level of fear. My co-workers and I scrambled into action, searching for the boy; in my head, I was praying for God to protect him and help us find him. Nearly two hours later, we found him playing in another area of the park. I was so relieved and so thankful he was OK. That may have been the longest two hours of my life.

I held several other jobs, including storekeeper, taxi driver, and delivery person, among others. But it was Mr. Haydon who knew I was capable of much more, and he encouraged me to pursue education as a means of finding a more satisfying job. I trusted his judgment and could feel his respect for me, so I listened to him and enrolled in night school. In

1971, at the age of thirty-two, I earned a high school equivalency diploma by completing the General Educational Development tests (or GED), spurring a long cycle of education whereby the more I learned, the more I achieved, the better I felt, the more motivated I was, and so on. Hard work had always been a necessary part of my life, and it was something I appreciated because in my youth, if I worked hard, I usually had something to eat! Now education was also a big part of my life.

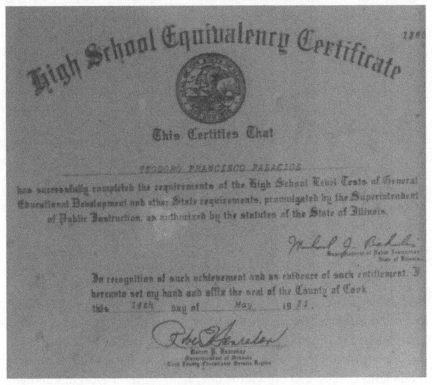

Teddy's GED (high school equivalancy) certificate
1971
(Photo courtesy of Teodoro Palacios Flores)

National Gymnasium in Guatemala City

Within a few years, several of my friends in Guatemala began raising public awareness about my basketball accomplishments. It all started because they had watched my successes over the years and felt my frustrations over the lack of support. A friend of mine who hosted a radio talk show on a station in Guatemala City started telling my story and encouraged his listeners to respond with notes and calls to their government officials, insisting that they formally acknowledge my achievements. Then another friend, Enrique Brémermann, who had a wrestling TV show, *Lucha Libre International*, did the same thing. The story caught on, and then several of my journalist friends from different newspapers in Guatemala also participated by writing articles. I felt so happy, so nostalgic, when I learned the public answered the call; pressure mounted from thousands of fans who had witnessed my successes and enjoyed my basketball games or who were just sympathetic to my plight. The authorities could no longer deny me. In 1972, they decided to formally rename the national basketball gymnasium to Gimnasium Teodoro Palacios Flores in my honor. Not only that, but they also cast a bust of me and placed it near the entryway. The bust was eventually stolen; I suppose someone loved me so much they wanted to look at me all the time!

I was living in Chicago when I received the phone call saying that the renaming ceremony would be taking place and that they wanted me to attend. Since I knew how much effort my friends put forth to make the renaming happen, I immediately accepted their invitation and made plans to attend the ceremony.

It was so surreal to walk up to the gymnasium and see my name emblazoned across the top. It puzzled me to think about how this could have happened—*to me*. It was as if my life had been a miracle. How else can it be explained that with my desperate, depressed, impoverished upbringing, I had achieved so much? I looked to the sky in wonderment, joy, and appreciation. I was immediately flooded with thoughts of my dear mother, my granny, and my aunt Felipa, along with the faces of hundreds of people who helped me and showed me kindness over the years; they were all with me that day as I stood in front of the gymnasium. I knew at that moment that I was blessed by God and that the glory for my success goes to him. I also felt I needed to do more, to help others find their way, and to inspire others to depend on their spiritual strength. It is the reason this book *had* to be written.

Although the bust is gone, the gymnasium still stands today and is host to a variety of events, including basketball, wrestling, and boxing exhibitions, as well as community and other indoor athletic events, many of which I have attended over the years. Back in the day, the ticket agents would recognize me, and they always seemed so honored, almost nervous, that I was there. Nowadays though, many people, especially the new generation, only know my name. When a ticket agent doesn't actually recognize me, I just buy a ticket to get in rather than make a fuss or embarrass someone for not knowing me. Sometimes when this happened, a supervisor at the event would get complaints from people who did know me and who saw that I bought a ticket. Inevitably, a manager would come over to apologize and convey how honored they were to have me at the gymnasium. Once I was recognized by the crowd, people would usually gather around me, ask me questions, or take a picture with me. At least my basketball career was finally acknowledged. I thought it would have triggered the Autonomous Sports Confederation of Guatemala to recognize my jumping career, but that did not happen.

I have always wished there would be a three-tiered award podium placed near the front of the gymnasium so that the next generation of athletes can symbolically follow in my footsteps. The interactive experience would involve three sets of bronze casts and look something like this:

1. Visitors could slip off their shoes and stand in a cast of my bare feet on the ground, demonstrating how I started jumping.
2. Next, they would walk up to the top of the podium and step into a bronze cast of my *tied* cleats to feel the glory of winning a gold medal, just as I did.
3. Finally, they would step back down on the other side into a bronze cast of my *untied* cleats, which would be my invitation for the next athlete to continue in my footsteps to achieve success for Guatemala or whatever country they represent.

Perhaps one day this dream can also become a reality.

Exterior of Gymnasium Teodoro Palacios Flores
Guatemala City
(Photo by Ana Leticia Molina Rivera)

Gymnasium Teodoro Palacios Flores
Guatemala City
(Photo by Catherine Palacios Bermudez)

Interior of Gymnasium Teodoro Palacios Flores
Guatemala City
(Photo courtesy of CDAG; by Ana Leticia Molina Rivera)

Teddy the Student

Obtaining my GED (high school equivalency) opened my mind, provided me with many opportunities, and allowed me to pursue more education. I was able to enroll at the Olive–Harvey College in Chicago, where I studied very, very hard. I studied with my soul, and I was so appreciative to get to go to school, so much so that I never missed class. I remember one day in particular that was freezing cold outside, probably around fifteen degrees below zero. Nonetheless, I started walking toward the campus a few blocks away, pushing through the wind with my head down and with the snow blowing hard against my bare face. When I got to the school, I went to class, and the only one in the room was Professor Lucy, who was more than surprised to see me. It seems I was the only student who showed up for her class during the heavy winter snowstorm. Impressed with my dedication, she invited me to sit and talk for a few minutes. She asked me, "Why in the world are you here in this blizzard?" I simply explained that my Aunt Felipa had taught me to be responsible, show up on time, and complete my duties. So I came to class, not knowing that people would not show up due to the weather. That day,

I instantly earned Professor Lucy's respect and appreciation because she saw my dedication and responsible ways. From then on, she was always willing to help and support me with schoolwork whenever I asked for her assistance. We had severe weather a few more times that year, but I did not show up at school, because I learned to listen to the radio for updates.

I loved going to school, learning, and being on the campus. I always had a job, but I never let my studies go—they were the priority. Between work and school, time passed quickly, and in 1976, I graduated with an Associate of Arts Degree. Once again, I found myself in a state of disbelief—me, Teddy, a college graduate, living in the United States of America. Never, ever as a youth or even as a young adult did I even imagine this was a possibility. Achieving this milestone only made me want more. I was so curious about the way the world worked, and I had so many questions. I had learned so much in the last few years, but I had to know more. Soon after, I enrolled at Chicago State University to continue my studies toward a bachelor's degree.

Teddy's Associate Degree in Liberal Arts
Olive-Harvey College, Chicago, Illinois; 1976
(Photo courtesy of Teodoro Palacios Flores)

That same year, 1976, my heart was broken when I learned the bad news that Guatemala had suffered a devastating earthquake. Thousands of Guatemalans had lost their homes, businesses, and all their belongings. I immediately started raising awareness by reaching out to my friends and the local Latino community. We collected food, clothes, and many other supplies to help our countrymen in need back in Guatemala. We were blessed to be able to send so many goods. Some government officials in Chicago noticed my great concern and dedication, and they were impressed with what I accomplished in the community. The City of Chicago recognized me with an award for advocating for the Guatemalan earthquake victims.

I stayed focused on my studies while still working late at night as a taxi driver. During my last year of classes, I was chosen as the best student of the university and was selected to be in the Who's Who Among Students in American Universities and Colleges program, which honors students who consistently demonstrate excellence. Sometime later, I learned that former US president John F. Kennedy had also received that award when he was in college. Even though our upbringings were polar opposites, I was amazed to know I had received the same award as a great world leader. Within just two years and after a lot of sacrifices, I earned a Bachelor's Degree in Bilingual Education in 1978.

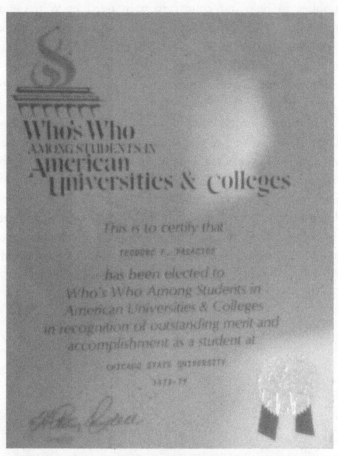

Teddy's Who's Who Among Students in American
Universities and Colleges certificate
Chicago State University
(Photo courtesy of Teodoro Palacios Flores)

Teddy's Bachelor's Degree graduation
Chicago State University, Chicago, Illinois,
United States of America; 1978
(Photo courtesy of Teodoro Palacios Flores)

Teddy the Teacher

Starting in 1979, I found my calling as a teacher when I began working as a bilingual professor at James H. Bowen High School in Chicago, followed by Pickard Elementary School in Chicago. Later I moved to Hubbard High School, and then I also taught night school at Kennedy–King College in Chicago.

Teaching made me happy, as it allowed me to motivate and inspire children and teenagers. Oftentimes, I would share stories of my life and how I had fought with all my heart and energy to become someone. I also became an advocate for poor children. I would say to every child that it didn't matter if they were from a very poor family. I explained that I didn't have a mother, a father, shoes, food, or a home, and that I worked very hard from a young age to survive, but that today, in Guatemala, the national gymnasium shines with my name. I know I touched many lives in Chicago.

Teddy teaching at Pickard School in Chicago,
Illinois, United States of America
(Photo courtesy of Teodoro Palacios Flores)

Teddy with students at an event for his accomplishments by Asobasquet
Guatemala, 1981
(Photo courtesy of *Prensa Libre*)

(Photo courtesy of Teodoro Palacios Flores)

However, soon after I first started teaching, I learned I would eventually need a master's degree to continue teaching. Despite the financial struggles and sacrifices, along with the academic rigor and working as a teacher, I was determined to earn a master's degree. I persevered and completed my master's in Bilingual Education from Chicago State University in 1983. I was very proud of this achievement. Once again, I found myself counting my blessings as I wondered how a homeless kid living in the streets of Puerto Barrios, Guatemala could wind up in the United States with a master's degree, teaching, leading, and inspiring others.

Summary of my educational achievements:
- GED, 1971 (State of Illinois in Chicago)
- Associate Degree in Arts, 1976 (Olive–Harvey College in Chicago)
- Bachelor's Degree in Bilingual Education, 1978 (Chicago State University)
- Master's Degree in Bilingual–Bicultural Education, 1983 (Chicago State University)

Teddy's Master's Degree graduation
Chicago State University, Chicago, Illinois,
United States of America; 1983
(Photo courtesy of Teodoro Palacios Flores)

Teddy's Master's Degree in Bilingual–Bicultural Education
Chicago State University, Chicago, Illinois,
Unites States of America; 1983
(Photo courtesy of Teodoro Palacios Flores)

My early years of traveling abroad to competitions with no support left a deep impression on me, something I never wanted a fellow Guatemalan to have to experience. For this reason, I found it to be a noble act and made it my self-imposed responsibility to be supportive of visitors whenever possible. Even without an ambassador's title, every time I was aware of a soccer team, a group of students (or even a single student), or dignitaries coming to Chicago from Guatemala, I was present and ready to assist them in any way I could. For example, I offered to help in simple ways, like giving someone my phone number so they could call to ask me questions or just have someone to talk to. I would tell people how to get around the city or help people find a place to live. Sometimes I would let people stay with me until they found their own place. Oftentimes, friends from Guatemala would come to Chicago to buy cars and drive them back to Guatemala to sell. In these cases, I helped by taking them to the right places and interpreting for them. It was always a treat to spend time with my countrymen, but I also enjoyed helping people regardless of where they were from. A lot of my free time was spent being a part of the community through volunteer activities, especially cultural or sports events.

Teddy's United States of America citizenship certificate
1987
(Photo courtesy of Teodoro Palacios Flores)

(Photo courtesy of Pixabay.com)   (Photo courtesy of Hector
Xutuc Castillo)

My United States Citizenship

The year 1987 was truly a milestone year for me. Studying was now second nature to me, and I was working hard on one specific test—the US citizenship test. On July 21, I became a citizen of the United States of America. What an honor, and I was able to maintain dual citizenship with Guatemala!

Order of the Quetzal

In 1998, the president of Guatemala came to Chicago, and I was part of the welcoming committee from city hall that went to receive him. He recognized me and was surprised to see I was there; he asked me how I had become part of that group. I explained that I was a member of the Sub-Commission of Human Rights for the mayor of Chicago, Richard Daley, and how it was personally important to me to be present any time a Guatemalan came to visit. Intrigued by my presence and dedication, he wanted to know more about me, asking for my resume, which I gave to him. He was shocked when he saw it.

Shortly after his visit, I received an invitation from the president to come to Guatemala to receive the Order of the Quetzal, Guatemala's highest award. This time, *I* was shocked! Flooded with emotions, I was surprised, overwhelmed, and happy that the government was finally going to recognize me. I thought back to the many times I won a medal, and I would see the flag and hear the Guatemalan national anthem playing as I stood on the podium to receive a medal for Guatemala. Even though it was years later, receiving the Order of the Quetzal award now still made the sacrifices worth it.

My students knew my spirit, as I had shown them many acts of kindness. In return, they showed me much love and respect, as did my colleagues where I was teaching at the time. I was so excited to share the news with them, and they were all so overjoyed for me, as they were fully aware of my story. I was beginning to feel the support.

The awarding date was set, and I went to the principal to request a few days off to return to Guatemala to receive the award. To my dismay, he denied my request. I was in disbelief; however, I couldn't afford to lose my job, and I refused to be disobedient. I notified my contacts in Guatemala that I could not get time off from work for the trip. This news outraged them, but they told me not to worry and that it would all work out.

A few days later, as the principal was coming out of his office at the high school, a group of reporters cornered him, praising him for having such a wonderful man on his staff and asking him for comments about me receiving the highest honor a country can bestow to one of its citizens. Anxious and insecure, he said he had no comment, and then he covered his face with his jacket and ran down the hall, hiding in the men's bathroom until they left. Now I'm not sure about this, but I bet he threw up while he was in there, as he was the nervous type. Now he knew he wasn't going to get away with his hasty decision to deny my request for a few days off. Soon afterward, the principal notified me that I could take the time off. This is another great example of the amazing power of the press and my friends, the reporters!

Back in the days when I competed, I would fly back to Guatemala with medals and trophies, but usually, no one would be waiting for me or even notice me. This time, however, when I arrived at La Aurora International Airport in Guatemala, it was a different story. A crowd of friends, reporters, and others had gathered to greet me. Although overwhelmed with appreciation, the biggest grin you can imagine appeared on my face. I quickly recognized several of them: Rubén Camas, Elma Elliott, Ernesto Milan, and Jorge Mario Guillen, to name a few. Smiles, handshakes, and hugs ensued, and it was a beautiful reunion. Good things truly do come to those who are patient and persevere.

A few days later, in Guatemala, I stood tall, proud, and strong at the ceremony in the National Palace, where I was presented with the medal of the Order of the Quetzal, in the grade of Grand Cross, the highest award in Guatemala. Gazing around the room, I saw many of my old friends, athletes, and reporters who knew me from my sporting days. The range of emotions I felt is nearly impossible to describe. I felt everything from elation and pride to confusion and sadness. Why were fans here now but not then? Why was there so little support for me when I was doing such a wonderful job for Guatemala? Why couldn't they have given me that thirty years ago?

Nonetheless, I relished the moment. At last, the recognition I had deserved and craved was about to be given to me. The room was filled with some of Guatemala's best athletes, including my great friend Mateo Flores, an avid runner who, in 1952, won the Boston Marathon and subsequently had the soccer stadium in Guatemala named in his honor. Interestingly,

Mateo and I have the surname Flores in common. Most people recognize that we are well-known Guatemalan athletes, but they get us confused since the *reason* we are famous is less publicized. It could also stem from the fact that our Guatemalan students are not taught to recognize the value of our people or our national heroes, including the efforts some of us have made to represent Guatemala. I would love to see this book become part of the required reading curriculum of our middle schools in Guatemala, because I believe there are many children who just need to know they are not alone in their struggles and they can still achieve success on levels that perhaps they don't even know exist. If that happened, I would see that as the full and complete recognition and support of my sacrifices and efforts.

They had organized a basketball tournament that day to pay homage to me at Gymnasium Teodoro Palacios Flores. The four teams were the national team, with players under twenty-two years old; the champion team, St. Francisco, from El Salvador; a combined team from the best players from a few states in Guatemala; and the team of Leones de Marte (where I used to play). It brought back such wonderful memories.

Teddy at the Order of
the Quetzal ceremony
(Photo courtesy
of CDAG)

Teddy with the Orden
del Quetzal
(Photo courtesy of CDAG)

While I was there, I met with a group of young athletes in Guatemala, and I advised them to practice the sport they love the most, but to never, ever abandon their studies. I still feel so lucky to have had great mentors who encouraged me to start my college studies, even though I was thirty-two.

A reporter asked me if it was true that I said the Order of the Quetzal should have been given to me over thirty years ago. "Yes," I said, "I represented Guatemala in many countries, receiving medals and trophies, and brought recognition to my country for many years, yet I never received anything from the government." They didn't even provide me with a uniform or proper shoes (or cleats). I remember in either Brazil or Chile, they didn't even give me a shirt or a jersey; I had to cut the sleeves out of an old T-shirt just to have something to wear for the competition. Oftentimes at events, I would look around at the other athletes, who were well supported, and I would wonder if they noticed me, without a uniform or shoes. As I mentioned previously, I used to dream of the day the Autonomous Sports Confederation of Guatemala would give me an official jacket with *Guatemala* written on the back of it in a semicircle, similar to what athletes from other countries had, but they never did. Many years later, I bought one for myself! To this day, I proudly wear the jacket, and underneath it is usually one of my many T-shirts with pictures or facts about my athletic career.

The year 1998 was a banner year. Shortly after returning to Chicago, I was surprised with another award—a beautiful resolution from the City of Chicago recognizing my achievements and comparing me with Michael Jordan. This, too, was a great honor. I lived about thirty years of my life in the beautiful city of Chicago, where I studied, worked, and contributed to many community activities.

(Note: Resolution transcribed for better readability)

Resolution

Sponsored by
**THE HONORABLE ROBERTO MALDONADO,
COUNTY COMMISSIONER**

WHEREAS, Guatemalan President awarded the legendary Guatemalan athlete and Chicago public school teacher, Teodoro Palacios Flores, the "Orden del Quetzal" at the National Palace of Guatemala on September 9th 1998, the most distinguished award given in Guatemala, and

WHEREAS, Palacios' rise to athletic fame began in the early sixties when he won almost every major high-jump competition in Latin America and soon became one of the best high-jumpers of the world, and

WHEREAS, Palacios has competed internationally in the Olympics, Pan American games, Central American and Caribbean games, winning numerous bronze, silver and gold medals, and

WHEREAS, Palacios has become the "Michael Jordan" of Guatemala, revered by all who know him and honored for his transcendent athletic ability with a national stadium and statute named in his honor, and

WHEREAS, it wasn't until after Palacios accomplished national and international recognition that he came to Chicago to pursue formal education, and

WHEREAS, at the age of 31 Palacios obtained his G.E.D. and then went on to receive an Associate of Arts Degree from Olive Harvey College, a Bachelor of Arts and a Master of Arts degree from Chicago State University, and has taken graduate courses at Northeastern University, Loyola University and the University of Chicago, and

WHEREAS, after touching the hearts of the people of Guatemala with his extraordinary athletic achievements, Palacios touched the minds of the youth of Chicago, teaching in the Chicago Public Schools for twenty years including Hubbard High School since 1990.

NOW, THEREFORE BE IT RESOLVED, that the President of the Cook County Board and the Board of the Commissioners congratulate Teodoro Palacios Flores on receiving the special honor of the "Orden del Quetzal," and

BE IT FURTHER RESOLVED, that a suitable copy of this Resolution be tendered to Mr. Teodoro Palacios Flores and to the Consul General of Guatemala, as a token of this Honorable Body's recognition and admiration.

Approved and adopted this 5th day of November, 1998

ROBERTO MALDONADO
Commissioner, 8th District

JOHN H. STROGER, JR., President
Cook County Board of Commissioners

Resolution from the Cook County of Chicago
Illinois, United States of America; 1998
(Photo courtesy of Teodoro Palacios Flores)

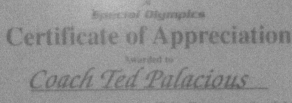

Special Olympics

Certificate of Appreciation

Awarded to

Coach Ted Palacious

whose interest, enthusiasm, and unselfish efforts gave Special Olympics athletes a chance to learn, a chance to know the joy of sports and athletic competition through participation in the

Special Olympics Program

Project 2000 of Soccer Clinic

October 10, 1997

(Photo courtesy of Teodoro Palacios Flores)

CHAPTER SEVEN

Back to Guatemala, Paying It Forward

Age Sixty-One to Present

After living about thirty years in the United States, about twenty-four of those years as an English high school teacher in Chicago, I returned to Guatemala in 2000 to live out my life and share my story with the next generation of Guatemalans, especially the children. With some friends, I founded a non-profit called FUNDE in the early 2000s, which allowed me to go to schools in the rural areas of Guatemala to motivate children and donate soccer balls, soccer shoes, and other sporting goods. My goal was to inspire the youth that lived in poverty and even those that lived with privilege. While others may not have seen it, I saw a lot of potential in those children, not just for sports but also for the arts, music, mathematics, and much more. Years later, due to some accounting discrepancies associated with the management staff of FUNDE, I decided to end the foundation, as I was not willing to allow any wrongdoing to be associated with or interfere with my dream of helping kids. Despite the dissolution of the foundation, I still devote my resources and time to helping children. Furthermore, I am continuing my mission through the publication of this book.

Non-profit founded by Teddy and friends
(Photo courtesy of Teodoro Palacios Flores)

Teddy at the Doroteo Guamuch Flores Soccer
Stadium, promoting FUNDE
(Photo courtesy of *Prensa Libre*)

(Photo courtesy of Teodoro Palacios Flores)

Nuestra Misión:

Incentivar y promover la práctica del deporte en la niñez y la juventud de escasos recursos, desarrollando en sus practicantes hábitos y valores tales como: Disciplina, constancia, respeto, solidaridad, patriotismo, etc. Así mismo, mejorar la calidad de vida de aquellos ex deportistas que en el pasado dieron gloria al deporte nacional y que, en la actualidad se encuentran en condiciones económicas precarias.

Nuestra Visión:

Coadyuvar a la formación de nuevos valores para el deporte nacional, especialmente en el área rural.

Izabal

Algunos Objetivos:

- Mejorar las condiciones de los niños y jóvenes de escasos recursos que practican deporte.

- Colaborar con el desarrollo del deporte, en sectores de pobreza extrema, con énfasis en el área rural.

- Contribuir a mejorar la educación integral de las y los niños y jóvenes guatemaltecos, con el propósito de promover una cultura de paz.

(Photo courtesy of Teodoro Palacios Flores)

(Photo courtesy of Teodoro Palacios Flores)

(Photo courtesy of Teodoro Palacios Flores)

(Photo courtesy of Teodoro Palacios Flores)

(Photo courtesy of Teodoro Palacios Flores)

(Photo courtesy of Teodoro Palacios Flores)

(Photo courtesy of Teodoro Palacios Flores)

(Photo courtesy of Teodoro Palacios Flores)

(Photo courtesy of Teodoro Palacios Flores)

(Photo courtesy of Teodoro Palacios Flores)

(Photo courtesy of Teodoro Palacios Flores)

(Photo courtesy of Teodoro Palacios Flores)

(Photo courtesy of Teodoro Palacios Flores)

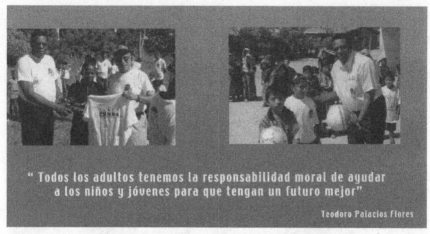

" Todos los adultos tenemos la responsabilidad moral de ayudar
a los niños y jóvenes para que tengan un futuro mejor"

Teodoro Palacios Flores

"We adults have the moral responsibility to help
children and young people have a better future."
(Photo courtesy of Teodoro Palacios Flores)

I was always so honored to be a motivational speaker at local events.
When I spoke to the audience, I didn't have to prepare for it; I just spoke
from the heart and told the story of my athletic and public life, just as
I have done here. People attended because they knew my famous name
and thought I was some kind of super jumper or superman (haha); they
rarely knew of the obstacles I overcame or how I persevered despite the
adversities. In one of my presentations in 2001 or 2002, the Guatemalan
president was in attendance. He literally began to cry out loud, as he had
never heard my story and could not believe what I endured. In fact, many
people have cried throughout my presentations.

One of my dreams is to build a museum in Puerto Barrios, which
would include the history of Livingston, Puerto Barrios and Guatemala,
as well as sections dedicated not only to my story but also to other athletes
and successful people from Izabal. I would also include exhibitions from
local artists and creative works of all kinds—all this to motivate and
demonstrate what is possible for the youth of Guatemala.

A Trip to New York City to Save My Vision

By 2011, I found it was becoming increasingly difficult for me to see, and I knew I needed to find out what was happening with my vision. The local doctors were unable to fix my problems, so in July 2011, I traveled to New York City to meet with a specialist to see if anything could possibly be done since I was becoming more blind every day. My good friend Juan Carlos Pocasangre, whom I met several years earlier through his volunteer work and humanitarian efforts within the community both in New York City and in Guatemala, made sure I saw a top ophthalmologist. Not only did Juan Carlos give me a place to stay in his house; his mother, Beatriz, also cooked delicious meals for us, and his entire family welcomed me in their home. I met his brother Olyver, his sister Betzy, his friend Milciades, and especially important to me, his nephew Anthony, who was too young to understand who I was, but I am sure he will learn about my story from his uncle. Juan Carlos also took a couple of weeks off work to take me to the doctor and other places where many local Guatemalans in New York City wanted to see me. It was amazing to spend the time with so many friends and others from back home in Guatemala. Overall, it was a wonderful trip, except for the news from the ophthalmologist; he declared me legally blind in one eye, without the possibility of repair. The news was disappointing, but I was not *completely* blind—I could still see with my other eye!

Beatriz Pocasangre, Teddy, Anthony, and Betzy Blancero
Brooklyn, New York City; 2011
(Photo courtesy of Juan Carlos Pocasangre)

The Order of Mateo Flores Award

The Order of Mateo Flores Award is an award named after my great friend. It is given to the national athletes whose accomplishments have put Guatemala in the global spotlight. I was honored to receive the Order of Mateo Flores Award in 2012, and it was especially sentimental because it was presented to me in the gymnasium bearing my name and was witnessed by many friends and reporters. It was great to read the newspapers the next day mentioning me as the greatest high jumper Guatemala has ever had. The article went on to say that I am a role model for the Guatemalan people, something I could not have imagined being in my younger years.

CHAPTER EIGHT

Remembering Close Friends

Mateo Flores

A great sports colleague and friend of mine, Mateo Flores (born Doroteo Guamuch Flores February 11, 1922–August 11, 2011), is another athlete who made Guatemalans proud. Many people get us confused because of our common surname, Flores, and the fact that we were both well-known athletes competing in international venues. Although we are not related, Mateo and I became the greatest of friends, keeping in touch frequently until his passing in 2011.

We have so much in common besides just our name: we were both raised very poorly, we are both well-known athletes from Guatemala, and we each have a sporting venue named after us in Guatemala. We were also both awarded the Order of the Quetzal. Like me, Mateo's athletic prowess probably developed as a result of his adversities and hardships. He worked for many years at a textile company located in El Guarda in Guatemala City. He used to run several miles to work every day, and after a long, hard day of physical work, he would run home to the county of Mixco, where he lived.

Mateo's son, Jorge Antonio Guamuch, recounted that one day his father's coworkers asked him to join their marathon running team, but he didn't want to at first. Eventually, he said yes, and the team started competing at local marathons. Since long-distance running had been a part of Mateo's daily routine for years, his stamina was incredible, so marathon running was a natural sport for him. Because of that, he did well—in fact, he did very well. It was the little taste of success he enjoyed in his early marathon competition that opened Mateo's eyes to what was possible. He started practicing very seriously, running from Mixco to El Mirador or farther up and then back to his house every day in the early morning, before work. It didn't take long for his running career to take off, and before he knew it, he was competing both locally and internationally!

Jorge remembers when his dad told him about one of his greatest competitions. He said he was in Mexico when he ran three marathons in one week, winning the gold medal in two races and the silver in the other one. People were in awe of his accomplishments, and the reporters said it was unprecedented. From this, he earned the nickname "Locomotive of the South." His son speaks very proudly of his father's great accomplishments. Mateo also won several national and international events:

1946 Central American and Caribbean Games in Barranquilla, Colombia
* Gold medal—10,000 meters
* Gold medal—half marathon
* Bronze medal—5,000 meters

1950 Central American and Caribbean Games in Guatemala City
* Silver medal—5,000 meters
* Silver medal—half marathon

1952 Helsinki Summer Olympics
* Part of the Guatemalan Sports Delegation

1952 Boston Marathon at the United States of America
* Gold medal—marathon
  Note: This was the highlight of his career and the most memorable marathon race. He won with a time of 2:31:53, nearly five minutes faster than the next finisher!

1954 Central American and Caribbean Games in Mexico City
* Gold medal—5,000 meters
* Gold medal—half marathon
* Silver medal—10,000 meters

1955 Pan American Games in Mexico City
  • Gold medal—marathon

Doroteo Guamuch "Mateo" Flores at the Boston Marathon
1952
(Photo courtesy of *Prensa Libre*)

Doroteo Guamuch "Mateo" Flores at his home in Guatemala
(Photo courtesy of *Prensa Libre*)

To commemorate such a great achievement, the Guatemalan government renamed the national stadium in his honor; it was then known as Estadio Nacional Mateo Flores (or in English, the National Stadium Mateo Flores), which was recently renamed Estadio Doroteo Guamuch Flores to correctly display his complete name. It is the largest multiuse national stadium in Guatemala, located in Guatemala City seating about 26,000 people. It was originally built in 1948 to host the 1950 Central American and Caribbean Games. Used mostly for soccer matches, the stadium has hosted the majority of the home matches of the Guatemalan national soccer team throughout its history. The venue is now operated by the Autonomous Sports Confederation of Guatemala.

I hope the facts about Mateo's world-renowned accomplishments will help people remember the differences between us. Even to this day, people do not realize who is who or what we did to receive recognition; nevertheless, they are happy to shake our hands and take pictures with us. We used to laugh when we talked about how people in Guatemala would get us confused all the time, and Mateo would say, "Can you imagine that? I am so short, and you are so tall!" Then I would say, "Hey, maybe it's because we are both so handsome."

Mateo brought great honor to Guatemala, and when he retired from competing, the Autonomous Sports Confederation of Guatemala responded. They agreed to provide him with a small percentage of the soccer game revenue from the stadium. Their contribution helped him make a living during his retirement, for which he was very thankful (Enrique Brémermann).

In the following pictures, it is easy to see who is who, and now it should be clear what each of us did for Guatemala, so happily and so proudly.

Teodoro "Teddy" Palacios Flores   Doroteo Guamuch "Mateo" Flores
(Photo courtesy of *El Diario*   (Photo courtesy of CDAG)
La Hora, Guatemala)

Left to right: Roy Fearon, Coco, Mateo Flores, Teddy,
Jorge Minera, Salomón Rowe, and Manolo Fearon
(Photo courtesy of CDAG)

I have been blessed with many great friends, such as those in this photo. Roy Fearon is considered one of Guatemala's greatest athletes, excelling in sporting events such as the triple jump, long jump, and 4×100 relay, in addition to soccer and basketball. A football stadium located in Puerto Barrios, Guatemala, bears his name.

Salomón Rowe, who competed in various jumping and track events, primarily during the 1970s and 1980s, won sixty-seven gold medals and was declared one of Guatemala's greatest athletes of the twentieth century.

Foto. CDAG. Guatedigital y APC-AV.

Salomón David Rowe Stewar, Doroteo Guamuch Flores y Teodoro Palacios Flores.

Salomón David Rowe Stewart (*left*),
Doroteo Guamuch "Mateo" Flores (*center*),
and Teodoro "Teddy" Palacios Flores (right)

Guatemalan national soccer stadium, Doroteo Guamuch Flores
(Photo courtesy of CDAG)

Guatemalan national soccer stadium, Doroteo Guamuch Flores
(Photo courtesy of CDAG)

Julio "El Caballo" Barillas

Throughout my life, I have had the honor of making many great friends, especially in the athletic community. One of those friends is Julio "El Caballo" Barillas, who was a talented and skilled athlete from Guatemala who competed in multiple sports. Julio competed in track and field events, breaking the records in Guatemala for the 100- and 200-meter races with times of 10.4 minutes and 22.0 minutes, respectively. He also competed in the 4×100 and 4×400 relays with solid results. He was given an award for being the fastest national athlete in Guatemala, which qualified him to compete in the track and field events of the 1952 Helsinki Olympic Games. Julio participated in track and field events in 1954 at the Central American and Caribbean Games held in Mexico City.

Julio also played basketball for many years. He played for professional teams, including Escuela Normal para Varones, Club Alacranes, and Club de Leones in the second division, where they were champions one year. Julio also played on the Guatemalan national basketball team.

Julio's talents extended to soccer, where his passion for the game and his fast footing helped his team win the championship in the second division, and afterward, they ascended to the first soccer division in Guatemala. He played with the first and second division soccer teams, including Mormones, Chichicaste, Ilgsa, Costa Rica, Auditoria, and Deportivo Escuintla.

Julio moved to New York City in 1970, about the same time I had moved to Chicago. We always made a point to keep in touch and visited each other on many occasions. Having a fellow Guatemalan athlete and friend in the US meant a lot.

In 1973, Julio and his wife, Melita Barillas, along with several of their local Guatemalan friends (including Faustino and Sheny Morales, Mario and Emma Chavarria, Jorge and Yoly López, and Ula and Rosa Maria Clara), incorporated the first Guatemalan nonprofit organization in New York City, named Guatemaltecos Unidos En Nueva York Inc. (GENY). Starting back in 1973 and continuing to this day, GENY represents Guatemala in the New York City Hispanic Day Parade, held on Fifth Avenue in Manhattan, every October for over forty-seven years. I had the honor of being asked by the members of GENY to be the grand marshal for the 2003 parade. It was an amazing event and so heartwarming to see the turnout of so many Guatemalans in New York City. Greetings to all the current members as well: Minor and Lili Gálvez, Hugo and Aida Calderón, Manuel and Magda Bolaños, Cesar and Alma Martinez, Luis and Sulma Mejia, and Juan Carlos Pocasangre.

Thanks to Julio's incredible knowledge about organizing sporting events, in 1974 he and a couple of his friends founded three soccer leagues: Liga Guatemala de Futbol, the Association of Ligas Hispanas de Futbol, and Liga Hispano–Americans de Futbol. Still today, the Liga Guatemala de Futbol is active, and players from various countries compete at the Red Hook Park in Brooklyn, New York City.

Luis Mejia, Julio and Melita
Barillas, and Teddy
at Restaurant Luna de Xelajú
Queens, New York City; 2011
(Photo courtesy of Juan
Carlos Pocasangre)

Melita, Teddy, and Julio
at the Hispanic Day Parade
Fifth Avenue, New
York City; 2003
(Photo courtesy of Melita Barillas)

(Teddy had many other great friends, but due to his health, we were unable to get the details to include them here.)

CHAPTER NINE

Reflections and Closing Thoughts

It took me a long time to realize what really happened to me, and to accept it. Even though I gave my life to Guatemala back in the fifties, sixties, and into the seventies, I was discriminated against by government officials in my own country, despite the fact that I brought honor to Guatemala with my diligence and dedication to sport and country. As it turns out, I did not portray the image that the political leaders of the time wanted for Guatemala, whether in terms of the color of my skin or because I was poor and somewhat uneducated in my early life, or all of that. Despite having endured countless events of discrimination over the years, I persevered to do my best, and in doing so, I honored my granny and my Aunt Felipa by following their advice and guidance. I also gave honor to my mother in heaven for being the son she would have been proud to call hers, and I have brought honor to my beloved Guatemala.

Many years later, after earning the right to be recognized, I was acknowledged through the naming of the gymnasium. I am also happy and honored to have a library in Amatitlán, a private school in Boca del Monte, and many other sports and community venues in Guatemala that are named after me. And of course, I finally received the Order of the Quetzal. Even though I am very appreciative of all the recognition I have since received, I will truly only feel at peace if once this book is published, it becomes part of the curriculum / required reading for our middle-school children in Guatemala. They desperately need to be exposed to real-life winners—people they can identify with and be inspired by. I am confident this book will do just that.

In May of 2014, I was finally recognized and rewarded by the Guatemalan government. I was officially declared Illustrious Guatemalan for all my national and international athletic and sports accomplishments. Moreover, they provided me with a monthly retirement pension of $1,025 (or Q8,000) for life, as they noticed I was in poor health and had a lot of medical and medicine expenses.

I can say with complete sincerity that there have been many improvements in the way athletes are supported. Today organizations such as the Autonomous Sports Confederation of Guatemala and the Olympic Committee have matured since my days of competition, and they provide more support to the athletes; however, there is still work to be done. I hope this book will bring attention to the absolute need for support of *all* competitive athletes, whether from Guatemala or any other country. I am living proof that with even just a small amount of kindness and support, a person can achieve much. Imagine what I could have accomplished with the proper support. With help and goodwill from people, we can collectively change lives and teach boys and girls and people of any age that they can reach their full potential, become champions, and be excellent citizens no matter where they live in the world.

I have visited over fifty schools in Guatemala where many children are hungry, without shoes, without a good home, and without school materials, and where the sports fields are in chaos. I have witnessed violence, drug addiction, and neglect of children's needs; and it deeply saddens me. Whenever possible, I gather a group of underprivileged children to tell them my story, to demonstrate the possibilities and give them hope. Invariably, their eyes brighten with curiosity as they listen and begin to identify with me. I tell them that each of them is God's creation, with unique and infinite potential, and that I see doctors, lawyers, teachers, engineers, coaches, athletes, and more. I tell them I have lived and suffered like them, saying, "Hey, I was like you. I had a poor life, but my values were strong. I remained respectful, I never took drugs, and I started my high school equivalency studies when I was thirty-one years old. It's never too late."

Teddy at a school, motivating children
Guatemala
(Photo courtesy of CDAG)

Teddy at a school, motivating children
Guatemala
(Photo courtesy of CDAG)

Teddy at Gymnasiun Teodoro Palacios Flores
Guatemala City, 2006
(Photo courtesy of Axel Vandenberg)

One of many T-shirts Teddy proudly wears all the time

CHAPTER TEN

A Few Short Anecdotes about Teddy

Contributed by Elma Elliott

I remember Teddy very well. The first time I remember seeing him was when I was about eleven years old, and I believe he was around thirteen years old. I lived within the same block of where he used to work at this bakery, and I used to see him making deliveries on a bicycle or with a basket. We never spoke other than to say hi to each other in passing every now and then, or sometimes when we were both at the basketball court shooting some hoops. At the time, all I knew about Teddy was that he was homeless. I had no idea he would become one of my great lifelong friends.

The year 1959 was memorable for two major reasons. First, to my pleasant surprise, I saw Teddy again in Guatemala City and also at the national gymnasium that is now named in his honor. By then, he was already an established high jumper who had started playing basketball. I remember he started with the basketball team Colosos in the first-division tournament and then moved to the major league team Leones de Marte. Teddy ruled when it came to catching all the rebound balls from the board or the basket. No one could match him on his jumps—he made it look so easy to get the ball. It was energizing to watch him play basketball and jump so high.

Second, the year 1959 was the year I was selected as Sportswoman of the Year. I had played with the women's national basketball team from age seventeen to twenty-two years old. The first time I went with the team to

Nicaragua, my parents had to sign an affidavit so I could go, because I was only seventeen years old. With me standing at 5'9", they used to call me "the Russian Tank" since I was very strong, and I was a lefty.

When I think of Teddy, I remember that he was very shy, probably due to his difficult childhood. But he remembered me, and then we spoke often at the gymnasium, where I played basketball for the women's national team and he was playing for the men's national team. Several times, Teddy and I were both part of the sports delegation that traveled to compete in a few countries like Costa Rica, Venezuela, and Panama. I was with the women's national basketball team that won the gold medal in the Central American Games in Costa Rica in 1960 and the silver medal at the games in Panama in 1962. At the 1960 games, Teddy was also there, playing with the men's national basketball team, and they won the silver medal.

Later, I moved to the United States to further my education. Through hard work and dedication, I achieved the following degrees:

- Bachelor of Arts (Brooklyn College, New York)
- Professional Diploma in Administration and Supervision (Fordham University, New York)
- Master of Education (Columbia University, New York)
- Master of Science in Education (City College of New York)
- Doctor of Education (Fordham University, New York)

While I was in school, I learned Teddy had moved to Chicago. It was great to know that a friend from back home was also in the United States and was also pursuing an education. We eventually connected and remained in contact over the years. When I heard he was to be given the Order of the Quetzal in Guatemala in 1998, I made sure to attend the ceremony. It was great to finally see him recognized and to see so many old friends and basketball colleagues. Over the years, there were many occasions we got together in Guatemala with friends, either at his house or mine, and reminisced about old times. Basketball may have been what initially bonded us as friends, but comradery and love of country kept us bonded.

Guatemalan women's and men's basketball teams
at the Central American Games
Women's team, gold; men's team, silver
Elma Elliott (*back row*), Teddy (*front row*)
San José, Costa Rica; 1960
(Photo courtesy of Elma Elliott; by Manuel Arévalo)

Left to right, standing: Mario Morales, Teddy, Manuel
De León, Esther Castañeda, Axel Vandenberg
Sitting: Neto Milan, Elba Salazar, and Elma Elliott
(Photo courtesy of Elma Elliott)

Contributed by Rodolfo Arana Flores

Teddy is my cousin, and it was always a thrill to see a newspaper article that said he had won a medal. As kids, we were so inspired by Teddy that we made up a high jump athlete game of our own; two of us would hold up a wooden stick, and the others would jump over it, just the way Teddy used to.

I remember when Teddy would come to Livingston to visit. Many of his cousins other kids and I were always so excited to see him. We would eagerly greet him and ask him about his great jumps that we saw in newspapers. He always seemed shy about it at first; however, as soon as he started telling us stories, his face would light up, and his voice would get more and more excited. We loved hearing about the people he met and the places he went. When he was in town, he would often come to friends' and family's parties. It was then that we would see him dance, and wow, he was a good dancer! Anything he did, from high jumping to dancing, we would imitate him. We all wanted to be just like Teddy.

One time when Teddy was in Livingston, he was watching a soccer game with his relatives and friends at a local soccer field. Folks were always stopping to say hello to him or ask about his trips and his competitions. He enjoyed telling stories about his life and competitions to everyone, but not in a boastful manner. As he was telling one of his high jump stories, a young man pleaded with him to show them how he did it by jumping the soccer goal. Not expecting they would find one, he *jokingly* said, "Well, guys, if I had a mattress to fall on so I wouldn't get hurt, I would do it," and continued with his story. Within forty-five minutes, a few trucks came rolling up, horns blowing, and some people were hooting and hollering, "Hey, Teddy, we have the mattress! In fact, we have three!" As always, Teddy smiled and was both surprised and pleased with the gesture. He did not disappoint them. He showed them where to put the mattresses and studied the bar, touching it with his hand and looking at it, making some jumping movements. Shortly, he did his thing, sailing over the top of the soccer goal. Everyone was so happy to have had the honor to see him jump.

Contributed by Axel Vandenberg

To talk about Teddy is to talk about a great athletic legend, both on *and* off the field. I have had the privilege of being his good friend since the 1960s, and we always kept in touch, even when he went to live in Chicago. I have never met a person with so much charisma and so much passion for inspiring and motivating others, especially children. Of course, for Teddy, it's so easy because the folks who know him—young, old, or in between—just love him. Others who only know his famous name are always enthused to meet him, shake his hand, and hear his wonderful stories about high jump and basketball. And of course, get a picture with him!

I have so many fond memories of Teddy. Early on, I saw him training for the high jump a few times, and it was beautiful to watch him soar in the air. I truly believe he was ahead of his time, as soccer was the main sport then (and still is today). The high jump event was not broadcasted on TV when he competed in other countries, so many Guatemalans were not even aware of the high jump sport or that Teddy was representing Guatemala or that he won so many medals. What's more, the government was not in tune with his great accomplishments either. It was only his close friends and a few people who read the newspapers that were familiar with news about his competitions and accolades.

Once, a group of friends and I were playing a basketball game called twenty-one on a court a few blocks from the national gymnasium. Teddy showed up carrying a trophy and a silver medal he had just won at the Pan American Games in Brazil, excited to share his victory with us. One of the guys said to him, "Hey, Teddy, put down those things and come play," and he humbly complied. At the time, we had no idea how big his accomplishment truly was or that he was continually competing with world-class athletes from Central and South America, Russia, the United States, and other major countries. We were just excited to see him and wanted him to join the game.

Mostly, I saw Teddy playing basketball, because I was also a basketball player. I played on the juvenile national team representing the state of Izabal, both nationally and internationally. Later, we both played on the national team of Maxibaloncesto, and because of our sporting achievements, we were among the most distinguished athletes of Izabal. In fact, we were the only two athletes from Izabal to be executive directors of the two major sports entities for basketball in Guatemala—Teddy was vice president of CONFEDE, and I was president of the Federación Nacional de Baloncesto (National Federation of Basketball). Watching Teddy play was incredible, especially when he dunked the ball. At that time, only two players in Guatemala could dunk the ball like the Americans did in the NBA—Teddy and our great friend Ernesto "Neto" Milan. We used to call Teddy the Kareem Abdul-Jabbar of Guatemala—that is how great he was! I remember one day several years ago, the Minister of Culture and Sports of Guatemala asked me *not* to bring Teddy to the events anymore, because people would focus on him and ignore the government officials! Of course, I just laughed about it, and so did Teddy.

Over the years, Teddy has always been a constant when someone needed help for a good cause, especially when it would benefit children. For example, a set of basketball hoops was donated to a school gym in Puerto Barrios, but I needed a truck and someone to transport them from the city, which would have been very costly. When I mentioned it to Teddy, he said, "Don't worry, let me make some phone calls." Before long, a truck with a driver showed up to handle the pickup and delivery. Teddy always knew who to call, and folks loved to help when he asked. He had a strong network of people, including the press, willing to do most anything because they knew he was a hero, even though in some cases, they might not have known how or why he was so renowned.

In 2010, Teddy called me because he wanted to celebrate the fiftieth anniversary of his high jump record in Guatemala by having a basketball tournament at the gymnasium bearing his name. Sadly, the Guatemala Autonomous Sports Confederation denied him the permit to do so. When I found out, I was so disappointed and wondered how that could be happening to Teddy again. He had brought so much honor to the Confederation and to Guatemala. I immediately called our friends, and we organized a basketball tournament in Puerto Barrios, Amatitlán, Quetzaltenango, and other places in Teddy's honor. Every event was filled to capacity, as people were enthusiastic to celebrate Teddy's amazing record of accomplishments with the living legend himself. Teddy was very happy too, and as usual, he owned the crowd and naturally gave many wonderful, motivating speeches, which he spontaneously delivered.

I believe Guatemala's Autonomous Sports Confederation did not want to celebrate the fiftieth anniversary of Teddy's world record because no one had broken his record up to that point, and they had not done much to improve certain sports in Guatemala, which would most likely have reflected poorly on the government. Nonetheless, Teddy and his high jump record were celebrated that day, giving the spotlight to a national hero who deserved the recognition and so much more!

Celebrating Teddy's fifty years of the national high jump record
Quetzaltenango, Guatemala; 2010
(Photo courtesy of Axel Vandenberg)

Left to right: Julio Sanchinelli, Jerry Slousher, Eliseo
Vargas, Teddy, and Axel Vandenberg
Guatemala national team of Maxibaloncesto
Las Vegas, Nevada, USA; 1993
(Photo courtesy of Axel Vandenberg)

Contributed by Juan Carlos Pocasangre

Back in 2011, Teddy came to stay with me so I could take him to the doctor for his deteriorating eyesight. I happily set the doctor's appointment, picked him up at the airport, and brought him to my home in Brooklyn, New York City, where I hosted him for a few weeks. It was an honor to spend time with such a humble man yet a great national hero, as I was aware of just some of his accomplishments and struggles for many years.

The first night he stayed with me, I remember him asking, "Pocasangre, do you have a radio? I cannot fall asleep without the AM radio station news playing at a low volume." He told me that many years ago, when he was living in a small room in Campo Marte Park in Guatemala, he had bought a simple clock radio to keep him company, and every night when he was ready to go to bed, he would listen to the news on an AM station to fall asleep. I was more than happy to set this up for him and made sure it was on an AM station because it has a unique sound. Just like back in Guatemala, he would fall asleep listening to it.

While I could say many, many wonderful things about Teddy, I mostly want to convey how humble and obedient he was. I observed how he followed the instructions of the doctors and waited patiently, hours sometimes, for the various examinations. He neither expected nor received special treatment, and that was how he wanted it.

During his stay, I took him to visit many Guatemalans in New York City, including a trip to the soccer fields at Red Hook Park in Brooklyn, which he enjoyed very much. Something very interesting happened just before one of the soccer games started. It's a story I love to tell, because it demonstrates Teddy's charismatic, unique style of communication and his ability to make people feel great.

We gathered in the middle of the soccer field to give Teddy an award from the Guatemalan group ASOVEGUA and friends, and to hear a few inspirational words from him, followed by a group picture. A Jamaican team was waiting for us to start the next game, but they became irritated and impatient because it was taking a few extra minutes. When Teddy realized that, he asked them, "Where are you from?" "Jamaica!" they yelled. A pleasant smile came over his face as he went closer to the players, and he said, "Ahhh, such a beautiful island. I was there in 1962 to compete in the Central American and Caribbean Games. Even though I won the gold medal, my very good friend Ernle Haisley won the silver medal. We were the best of friends since we had met years before in other competitions in the United States. You should be very proud to have had such a great Jamaican man represent your country for so many years and to have won so many competitions for your people."

Talk about flipping a situation from bad to good in an instant! What a great feeling it was to see all eleven Jamaican players smiling with pride as they praised Teddy with comments like "You're cool, man." To the rest of us on the field, they said, "Take as long as you need with this man."

Others recognized him and came to shake his hand and hopefully get a picture with him. In his normal fashion, Teddy began doing what he did best—motivating people who listened to his stories.

Teddy giving a motivational speech
Red Hook Park soccer fields, Brooklyn, New York City; 2011
(Photo courtesy of Juan Carlos Pocasangre; by Olyver Pocasangre)

Ladies from ASOVEGUA: Carmen, Ana, Carmen, Teddy, Betty
Red Hook Park, Brooklyn, New York City; 2011
(Photo courtesy of Juan Carlos Pocasangre)

Olyver Pocasangre, Teddy, Beatriz Pocasangre, Juan Carlos Pocasangre
2011
(Photo courtesy of Juan Carlos Pocasangre; by Milciades Melendez)

Juan Carlos and Teddy
Manhattan, New York City; 2011
(Photo courtesy of Juan Carlos Pocasangre)

CHAPTER ELEVEN

A Message from Me to You

Thank you for letting me share with you my experiences and jumps. I hope you are inspired to do your best, to achieve your dreams, and to persevere in the most difficult times, realizing that you can do far more than you ever think you can or that you even know exists. There will be silent times (the night sky), injustices (no shoes for a competition), discriminations (the woman wiping the phone and the Baltimore bar incident), lack of support or recognition (no band waiting or special awards upon returning), and trials of various sorts (denial for time off); but do not give up. *Persevere.* Turn to God, find your faith, and trust that God has a purpose for your life; there you will find your spiritual strength to propel you through your earthly trials.

There were men and women who took pity on me and who acted in kindness toward me, for which I am so very grateful. There are still so many good people in the world. If you have food to eat, shelter, and a loving family, never take it for granted. Stay in school and learn as much as you can, no matter your age or background. Achievement does not come easy. There will be pain or difficulties, but the payoff is worth it.

Keep reaching for the stars. It was my dream to be the best soccer goalkeeper in Guatemala at one time. God had a different plan for me. I achieved being the best high jumper in Guatemala and many countries. I was also a great basketball player, and today people play basketball and other sports in a stadium that bears my name. Years ago, walking down the dusty street in Guatemala as a homeless teenager with only a few years of elementary education, I would have never imagined I would become a teacher with a Master's Degree in the United States or would receive the Order of the Quetzal. How amazing all this is to me. How amazing it will be for you too.

Can you achieve your goals?

Absolutely. First, you have to set a goal, and then persevere. Here are a few recommendations that helped me reach my goals:

- Keep absolute faith and trust in God and his plan for your life.
- Ground yourself in strong principles, values, and ethics.
- Always follow instructions, be obedient, and have patience.
- Practice humility, find discipline, and endeavor to persevere.
- Do not use drugs or narcotics of any kind, and do not abuse alcohol.
- Avoid violence on all levels.
- Feel love for your homeland.
- *Never* give up in the face of adversity.

I want the jumps in your life to be even higher than mine.

Teddy at his home in Guatemala City
(Photo courtesy of Catherine Palacios Bermudez)

(Photo courtesy of *El Diario La Hora*, Guatemala)

Timeline of Achievements

YEAR	LOCATION	ACHIEVEMENT
1958	Mexico	Gold medal and a new record, III Encuentro del Club Venado (A Mexican athlete gave me a pair of shoes to use, as I was shoeless.)
1958	Guatemala	The military's first-class sports medal
1959	Venezuela	Gold medal, Central American and Caribbean Games
1959	Chicago, USA	Fourth place, III Pan American Games
1960	Quetzaltenango	High jump record; Xela, Quetzaltenango, Guatemala (2.10.5 meters, held for fifty-seven years until 2017)
1960	Chile	Gold medal, Ibero-American Games
1960	Chile	Two gold medals and, in one competition, the record of being the first athlete in South America to jump over two meters
1961	New York City, USA	Bronze medal, World Championship Indoor Competition, Madison Square Garden (organized by the New York chapter of the Knights of Columbus)
1962	Jamaica	Gold medal, Central American and Caribbean Games
1962	Spain	Gold medal, Ibero-American Games
1962	Germany	Gold medal, America vs. Europe Games
1962	Panama	Bronze medal, Guatemalan national basketball competition
1963	Boston, USA	Silver medal (the gold medal was won by John Thomas of USA)
1963	Toronto, Canada	Bronze medal

1963	Philadelphia, USA	Bronze medal
1963	Baltimore, USA	Gold medal
1963	Brazil	Silver medal, Pan American Games
1964	Michigan, USA	Certificate of Proficiency in English; English Language Institute, University of Michigan
1966	Puerto Rico	Gold medal, Central American and Caribbean Games
1967	Mexico	Gold medal; Jalapa, Veracruz, Mexico; I North and Central American Games (NORCECA)
1968	Mexico	Flag carrier with the Guatemalan delegation, Summer Olympic Games
1960–1968	Guatemala	Basketball champion for several years, major league division (Team: Los Leones de Marte)
1969	Guatemala	Basketball champion, major league division in Guatemala (Team: Hercules)
1970	Panama	Silver medal, Central American and Caribbean Games
1971	Chicago	Received GED (high school equivalency certificate), Illinois; took preparation classes at Jones Commercial High School, Chicago
1971	Guatemala	Declared Favorite Son of Livingston, Izabal
1972	Guatemala	National gymnasium named in my honor, Gimnasio Teodoro Palacios Flores
1976	Chicago	Received an Associate Degree in Arts; Olive–Harvey College, Chicago, Illinois

1976	Chicago	Awarded recognition from the City of Chicago for advocating for the Guatemalan earthquake victims
1978	Chicago	Included in the book *Who's Who Among Students in American Universities and Colleges* while attending Chicago State University
1978	Chicago	Graduated with a Bachelor of Science in Bilingual–Bicultural Education, Chicago State University
1983	Chicago	Graduated with a Master of Science in Bilingual–Bicultural Education, Chicago State University
1987	Chicago	Became a citizen of the United States of America
1996	Chicago	Thank-you certificate, Chicago Public Schools Teacher Appreciation Day
1998	Chicago	Resolution from the City of Chicago comparing me with Michael Jordan
1998	Guatemala	Order of the Quetzal, Grade of Great Cross (the highest honor awarded in Guatemala)
2003	New York City, USA	Grand marshal for the delegation of Guatemaltecos in New York, GENY, at the Hispanic Day Parade on Fifth Avenue
2004–2008	Guatemala	Honoree Ambassador of Sports
2004–2008	Guatemala	Senior Advisor to the Minister of Culture and Sports, as well as for the Confederación Deportiva Autónoma de Guatemala (referred to as the Autonomous Sports Confederation of Guatemala in this book)

2010	Guatemala	Boulevard in Puerto Barrios, Izabal, named in my honor (Teodoro Palacios Flores)
2010	Guatemala	Honoree at the City of Quetzaltenango celebration of the fifty-year anniversary of the national record for high jump (which I established in 1960)
2013	Guatemala	Order of Mateo Flores (Doroteo Guamuch Flores), given to athletes who represent Guatemala throughout their sports career

I won many more competitions, both at home and abroad, but I was not able to include them without specific dates and places.

Major Influencers in My Life

INFLUENCER	EXPLANATION
Carlota Flores de Palacios	Mother, died in 1941 when I was two.
Alejandro Palacios Nuñez	Father.
Catarina Nuñez de Palacios	Paternal grandmother who served as my surrogate mother after my mother passed away. She died in 1947 when I was eight.
Aunt Felipa Flores	My mother's sister who raised me after my grandmother died, until I was ten and a half.
Father Santiago	Catholic priest who offered me food, a blanket, and my first soccer ball.
Rafael Palencia	Owner of a bakery who taught me to bake, giving me confidence and a regular job.
Mr. Moncho	Bought me my first pair of soccer shoes and a sweater.
Colonel Luis Alfredo Ruano	The commanding colonel at the base in Puerto Barrios who recognized my talents for soccer and became my mentor.
Cyril Thomas	Army trainer who convinced me to try other sports, which was how I discovered my excellence in high jump and eventually basketball. Mr. Thomas was also my coach and mentor during my high jump career.
Ellwood Johnson	A trainer at a university in Pennsylvania who secured a scholarship for me to train with him for a year and who let me live in his home so that I could prepare to compete in the 1964 Olympics in Tokyo.

Ted Haydon	A coach from the University of Chicago whom I had encountered in many competitions in the United States and who, in the 1970s, was responsible for helping me get to the United States to find work and get an education. He sent an airplane ticket and wrote a letter to the United States Ambassador in Guatemala on my behalf.
Noél Illescas Palacios	My basketball mentor and trainer who actually taught me the rules and strategy of how to play basketball.

While they might not be called out here by name, there are many others—including family, friends, fans, acquaintances, athletes, and even strangers—for whom I am so appreciative, for the support, generosity, contributions, kindness, and friendship offered to me during some of the darkest days of my youth, as an aspiring athlete, and as an adult learner who knew little about the world.

Have a Story to Share?

Teddy touched the lives of many, and if you are one of those special people, we want to hear from you. Please post your stories, thoughts, or well-wishes on _____.

These links below show the medals summary table, which includes Teddy's winnings in different competitions.

https://en.wikipedia.org/wiki/Athletics_at_the_1959_Central_American_and_Caribbean_Games

https://en.wikipedia.org/wiki/Athletics_at_the_1962_Central_American_and_Caribbean_Games

https://en.wikipedia.org/wiki/Athletics_at_the_1966_Central_American_and_Caribbean_Games

https://en.wikipedia.org/wiki/Athletics_at_the_1970_Central_American_and_Caribbean_Games

https://en.wikipedia.org/wiki/Athletics_at_the_1963_Pan_American_Games

https://en.wikipedia.org/wiki/1960_Ibero-American_Games

https://en.wikipedia.org/wiki/1962_Ibero-American_Games

While this book was in the final stage of production, sadly Teddy passed away peacefully in Guatemala on August 17, 2019. It was his final dream to have this book published.

Many people have helped make this book a reality, either by providing pictures, stories, or research. For this, as well as for those who have read and will share Teddy's story, we are very thankful and appreciative.

Best wishes, Juan Carlos